A PROFOUND MERCY

Finding Redemption in the Despair of Our Own Doing

TODD MORRISON

Pacelli Publishing
Bellevue, Washington

Cover designed by Rachel Ronan, KiwiCreative.com
Author photo by Justin Lane
Interior designed by Pacelli Publishing

Scripture quotations marked (NLT) are taken from the Holy Bible, New Living Translation, copyright © 1996, 2004, 2007, 2013, 2015 by Tyndale House Foundation. Used by permission of Tyndale House Publishers, Inc., Carol Stream, Illinois 60188. All rights reserved.

Published by Pacelli Publishing
9905 Lake Washington Blvd. NE, #D-103
Bellevue, Washington 98004

Printed in the United States of America

ISBN 10: 1-933750-86-3
ISBN 13: 978-1-933750-86-6

CONTENTS

DEDICATION

For Kara, Grace, Sophia and Elizabeth--the strongest women I know. Thank you for your unconditional love; your strong truth; all your words; and your unending support of me and this project. I love you, my family, more than you could possibly know!

FOREWORD

Todd Morrison is a hero. I first met Todd in 1994 when he attended a youth pastor training session I was hosting in Southern California. He was a young youth pastor with an amazing story of redemption and grace. But back then he wasn't sure how to tell that story or whether he even wanted to tell it. He felt his story played more like a smear on his record than an example of profound redemption--especially in evangelical Christian circles. Since that time Todd has achieved great heights and profound lows. Those lows, as you'll read in this book, involve betrayal, great loss, addiction and recovery. Still, Todd's story has a redemptive quality that offers mercy to all who are broken. If you have ever needed grace or the assurance that your life matters, this book is for you. After reading this story, it's not a stretch for the rest of us to conclude that if God rescued Todd, he can most certainly rescue me!

Most all of us come from dysfunctional families but some are more dysfunctional than others. On a scale Todd's family was more dysfunctional than most. I believe you either repeat or recover from your negative family background. With an understanding of a profound mercy Todd chose to do the hard work of recovering. This true story reads like a novel and yet, my takeaway is more about the depth of grace and mercy of God and a man who persevered.

--Jim Burns, PhD
Author, Speaker and President of HomeWord
San Juan Capistrano, California

PART I
ADDICTION

THE END FROM THE BEGINNING

I first read these words by my late friend and best-selling author Brennan Manning when I was a twenty-four-year-old youth pastor who thought I knew much more than I did:

"Often I have been asked, 'Brennan, how is it possible that you became an alcoholic after you got saved?'
"It is possible because I got battered and bruised by loneliness and failure, because I got discouraged, uncertain, guilt-ridden, and took my eyes off Jesus. Because the Christ-encounter did not transfigure me into an angel."
– Brennan Manning, *A Ragamuffin Gospel*

I had not yet met Brennan, but that didn't keep me from casting judgment. That he was weak enough to succumb to alcoholism was a mystery to me. It was a deep stain on what had been my very high opinion of him. How could he lack the will power to resist a drink? He was a Christian, for crying out loud! Didn't that preclude him from becoming an alcoholic? No, it did not. I did not know enough about life, faith or forgiveness to judge Brennan's life. I was a self-righteous hypocrite, but I desperately lacked the awareness to recognize it.

I viewed alcoholics and addicts as less-than-whole people who were weaker than most--by their own doing. I was quick to offer the same judgment many Christians cast on those we think are cursed with an inferior station in life. Those children of a lesser god who wrestle with demons and darkness the rest of us have been blessed to avoid. Which, of course, we often take credit for avoiding--making it easy for us to legitimize our judgment.

Addiction and brokenness simply don't factor into the experience in many of our Christian circles. It's too messy and too frightening. Yet, we can't escape this truth: we are all broken, Christian or not, addict or not. No matter how we've attempted to suppress or avoid our brokenness, we are desperate to have it healed. Fearing it will never be healed, and terrified of the rejection we will face if discovered, we hide our brokenness behind the very best projections of our preferred selves.

Twenty years after first reading them, I was in a very different place when I read Brennan's alcoholic confession from a park bench in Rancho Mirage, California. I was a newly welcomed guest at the Betty Ford Addiction Treatment Center. I was broken, alone and desperate for hope, and I was terrified that my life, my career, and quite possibly my family would not be there for me when I got out. Brennan's words had taken on a whole new meaning in my life. They had become my very painful and very personal experience. I could no longer pass judgment on those I once viewed as inferior. I was now numbered among them.

It all started with a single back injury, which led to multiple surgeries. As the top opiate prescriber in the state of Washington, my doctor was offering narcotics to treat everything from depression and anxiety to pain and writer's block (truly, to help "open the creative process" for a few of his patients). His license would ultimately be revoked; but I never had trouble getting what my denial called a "legitimate prescription" for pain.

Just a month before going to Betty Ford, I finished my role as the transitional pastor at a large church in the Seattle area. A congregation whose glory years were a distant speck in the review mirror when its leadership asked me to step in and attempt to lead a "turnaround." It was a church in sharp decline--hemorrhaging people, money, and morale at a world-class pace. My closest friends warned me not to take the job. "You don't want 'administered the death of a church' on your resume," they said. But the risk-taker in me could not resist the challenge. After all, churches of a thousand people are not dying, they're just sick.

We did not need to close that church down. Within six months, new people started coming; the finances went from red to black and morale was on the rise. We cast a compelling vision and did the necessary work to be in the position to hire a permanent lead pastor after just thirteen months. That church is now thriving. By all accounts this was an uncommon success story.

I was thrilled to have led that turnaround and proven my friends wrong. But when my work was done, I had no idea what was next for me. It was a profoundly hollow experience to leave a place I had poured my heart into at the very time it was seeing success and growth. Success that I could easily have taken responsibility for! It wasn't long before fear set in and I found myself *"battered and bruised by loneliness and failure . . . I got discouraged, uncertain, guilt-ridden, and took my eyes off Jesus."*

I was suddenly a stay-at-home dad to our newborn daughter, Elizabeth. I missed the absolute gift that experience could have been because I was medicating my pain with hydromorphone (dilaudid). It did not take long for my wife, Kara, to suspect I had relapsed. My addiction has run my beautiful wife through a gauntlet of pain that I will never be able to undo. The fact that she continues to partner with me is a testament to who she is, and to God's grace. Kara became convinced I had relapsed when I hid the results of a tox-screen performed at a visit to the emergency room. I had gone to the ER believing I had some medical issue like mononucleosis or pneumonia. I was exhausted and not breathing well, but it wasn't because I was ill. I had potentially deadly amounts of hydromorphone in my system, depressing my breathing and profoundly impacting my judgment. My mind was so fogged up that I could not put together that I felt the way I did because I was slowly killing myself with copious amounts of pain meds--which I kept hidden in a pill bottle labeled "prednisone" so no one would discover it. Even with all I was doing to hide it, I was clueless as to just how consuming and lethal my disease had become. Such is the power my addiction had over my thinking and my life.

I couldn't simply stop taking the meds because that would have thrown me into debilitating and tortuous withdrawals. Still, hiding my addiction from my loved ones was tormenting. So much so that I found great relief in being found out. I was exhausted and taking so much hydromorphone that I am convinced I would have accidentally killed myself if it had gone on much longer. The mere possibility that the madness might soon end moved me from deep despair to a place of hope. I no longer had excuses, or the title "pastor" to keep me from getting the help I so desperately needed.

*****

Back in my twenties, I pleaded with God to break the chains of brokenness, pain and addiction that had plagued my family for generations. I experienced my family's wreckage up close and personally as a kid and its impact on me was far deeper than my younger self could have possibly known. Despite my pleading, God chose not to spare me from a disease that had plagued my father, his father and his father's father. Addiction is a family disease--and that is tragic on so many levels.

There were many times in my untreated addiction, which I refer to as the "lost years," that I believed God had abandoned me. I couldn't blame him because I was convinced that I deserved it. I believed if I had been a better person, he may have spared me the pain of this disease. I used my disillusionment with God, my low self-worth, and my chronic back pain as excuses to medicate my emotional pain and fuel my addiction.

*****

I was the only pastor at the Betty Ford Center, believe it or not. The first few days I was there, other "guests" would ask me what I did for a living. When I told them I was a pastor they replied, "You're a what? Pastor? *And you are here?!?!*" That was awesome.

I quickly, and quite easily, bonded with a SpaceX engineer, a doctor from Beverly Hills, and an actor most of us would recognize from his many film and television roles. My roommate was the only gay man in our "dorm," which was not easy for him. While our circumstances were different, we both needed to rebuild the trust we had broken with our spouses. The late-night wisdom and insights he shared with me were priceless. I found common ground with these guys. Our paths would never have crossed in the real world, but in treatment we shared so much--a common disease, our unique stories, much needed laughter, and a healthy amount of tears. It is amazing how the shared disease of addiction, and the desire to beat it, can turn disparate strangers into fast friends who desperately need each other to survive.

The treatment experience was sobering on many levels. Not only was I being treated for a disease that pastors are not supposed to have, I was doing it over the Christmas holiday--which was utterly depressing but also quite effective. I quickly came to realize that the more sophisticated addict plans his or her treatment *around* the holidays not *during* them. The place cleared out on December twenty-third. Only the worst of us would spend Christmas in treatment. My journal entries from those late December days repeatedly read, *"Don't ever forget where you are this Christmas or why you are here.*" I confess that forgetting is far too easy.

I nearly ruined my marriage and lost my family to this relapse. Still, I learned a life-altering lesson in treatment that Christmas. Something I'd been preaching and believing was true for everyone else for years: God does not often spare us from the pain or despair we would prefer to avoid in this life. But he loves to rescue us while we are *experiencing* pain and despair. He even rescues us while we are in the despair of our own doing.

Each day at the Betty Ford Center, I sat on that same bench and gazed up at the San Jacinto Mountains, certain my days in ministry were over. How could God possibly have use for someone as broken, flawed, and insidious as me?

I am far from the only Christian who has attempted to keep their brokenness in the shadows while casting the image of a much healthier self to the world around them. I am far from the only pastor who has battled the disease of addiction in secret and in silence. Too many pastors fear that being honest about their brokenness and asking for help will get them fired. Their problems would go from bad to worse as they would find themselves unemployed and still every bit as broken as before telling their truth. Unfortunately, this is not an unfounded fear. Sadly for them, their families, and their churches, they are stuck in a tragic spiral as they suffer in silence with a disease that wants them dead.

My favorite person in treatment was Aaron, a thirty-one-year-old engineer from Texas. Aaron was brilliant, charming, good-looking, and hilarious. Everybody loved him. I could never beat him at backgammon, even when he wasn't really trying. I had the privilege of meeting Aaron's parents during the family day visit. They loved their son deeply and were seeing him through his fourth stay in treatment. Aaron suffered so profoundly from the effects of alcoholism that his body was breaking down as though he were eighty-one rather than thirty-one.

Aaron and I talked about many things, including spirituality, our favorite bands, religion, and faith. His parents possessed a deep faith in Jesus but, like so many who battle addiction, Aaron turned away from God and the church about the time alcoholism took control of his life. Surprisingly, Jesus got some instant credibility with Aaron because a pastor (me) was in rehab with him. I didn't see that coming. As we exchanged stories at lunch one day, I felt compelled to say, "Aaron, you have to beat this disease, man! The world needs you. You have so much to offer." He smiled, unconvincingly, and said, "Yeah, I know."

Aaron left treatment shortly after I did. Within a few months he had started drinking, been arrested for public intoxication, and died as a result of his relapse.

Aaron's death created a shock wave of grief and disbelief that sent others from our group into their own relapses. I called my friend Sam in Denver, who had also been close to Aaron. "I couldn't deal with it, man," he said. "I had to drink. It hurt too much. But I think I'm okay." I hope that is true. I haven't heard from Sam since.

Addiction is an incurable disease. It never goes away, not ever.

Experts in addiction and recovery will tell you that it is a "progressive disease." It never gets better. If you stop drinking or taking drugs for a while--you have not hit the reset button. If you start again, even after years of sobriety, you will very quickly find yourself deeper into the disease than you have ever been. Tragically, even those who believe their rock bottom could not possibly have been lower, quickly discover when they start again, how much lower it can go. That's what happened to my friend Aaron, and alcoholism killed him.

Recovery is certainly achievable. But only with continued treatment through something like a twelve-step program and support from family, friends and a community that embraces you. For many that community is an Alcoholics Anonymous group and/or a faith community.

I struggled profoundly with owning the fact that I had this incurable disease. In my circles as a "professional Christian," addiction is mostly viewed as sin and often judged severely. All disease is the result of sin in the world. Yet it is very difficult for many evangelical Christians to see and understand addiction as disease (myself included). I have had family members tell me that I am simply weak-willed and that I don't trust God enough in this area of my life. Interestingly, they say that just after telling me I compartmentalize too much.

I have been in the room when colleagues have made unfortunate comments about those in the church who were suffering from various addictions, not knowing what I would never tell them: *I am that person you are judging.* All of this, along with my strong belief that I could control an uncontrollable disease, made it years before I came to grips with the life-long commitment I would have to make to my recovery. It was painful and humiliating for me to acknowledge that I was an addict. But the community I have discovered with others in recovery is pure grace.

It turns out that God uses those of us who are flawed and broken to do his best work: bringing his grace to people who need it as much as we do. Sharing my story with others has been tough for me at times. It is far easier to share my brokenness from twenty years ago than to share the lingering brokenness I still carry and will carry the rest of my life. Sharing this chapter with you causes me to feel more vulnerable than I'm comfortable with. Yet, to share my story is to offer people imprisoned by the chains of addiction and/or brokenness, as I have been, the opportunity to come out from the shadows of fear, despair and self-hatred so God can break the chains and heal the pain--at least I hope it does.

If you are acquainted with addiction, it may be terrifying for you or your loved one to even consider asking for help. There will most likely be people in your life who never understand addiction as disease. These same people will likely fail to see the sacred beauty within you. Do not give them space in your head or power in your life. Which is much easier said than done. Still, you are enough in God's eyes, as you are today, not as you or anyone else thinks you should be. Your life is worth recovering and it is most definitely worth living to its fullest.

We are never too late, too broken, too addicted, too isolated, too humiliated, too abandoned, or too forsaken for God to rescue us. As long as we have breath there is hope. God or, if you prefer, your higher power, doesn't just rescue us in our pain and brokenness--he redeems our pain and brokenness! He turns it into something that is good for us and beneficial to the people in our lives. He does this because he is love and he loves us. He does this because he absolutely delights in changing our lives for the better. So much so that he "rejoices over us with singing!" Yes, even you. God delights in *you*!

While I am known for being vulnerable and having a transparent style, I am only as transparent as I want to be. Just look at my Facebook posts. I am just now beginning to be truly vulnerable as I share this part of my story. I confess to feeling quite exposed about doing so. I know there are people in my various circles who will not understand and are likely to judge me. In fact, when I shared this manuscript with reviewers, most gave me great constructive feedback. However, there were a few, whom I counted as valued friends and colleagues, who surprised me with their interpretation and judgment--of me and of my motivation for writing and sharing this story. Yet, I'm thankful for their feedback. They helped me write a better story. Sharing has hurt my career, as a few of those colleagues "put me on the shelf" and isolated me, because of their interpretation of my motives. Some felt betrayed that I didn't divulge this information sooner. I get it. But to them I would say, "If you had diabetes, would you feel compelled to lead with that and to be defined by your disease?" Neither would I.

PART II
LIFE STORY

WHERE IT BEGINS

My childhood, as I look back on it, seems to belong to someone else--someone whose future held greater hope and promise than what unfolded throughout my life. Someone who would be spared the damage of experiencing profound betrayal, abandonment, loneliness--and the damage done to my childhood heart by those who were supposed to protect it. It is said that time heals all wounds. God's grace heals the deepest of wounds, but evidence of those wounds often lingers, as a reminder of that grace. While that may be true, I move through life with a pronounced limp.

My parents, Albert and Karen, were married at twenty, had me the day before their first anniversary, graduated from Moody Bible Institute in Chicago at twenty-two, and were sent out as missionaries by The Moody Church at twenty-three. Some of my earliest memories are of spending summers on the church camp circuit in Illinois, Wisconsin, and Michigan where my parents were the featured Bible teachers in "kids chapel." While the adults were treated to the big-name preacher in the main chapel, my parents were teaching their children.

When we weren't touring camps, my parents hosted a neighborhood outreach called Five-Day Club. Each afternoon my parents would send me out to invite all the neighborhood kids to our house for what I told them would be an opportunity to hear about Jesus. If they showed up, they were treated to the type of Bible story they might hear in Sunday school, most often taught by my mother. After the story, they were presented with the gospel and asked if they would like to ask Jesus into their hearts. I remember the whole thing being kind of fun. We always had ten or twelve kids who really seemed to enjoy it. It was a different time. It was a light ask Monday through Thursday. The big push happened on Friday afternoon--which was the day I "asked Jesus into my heart."

In today's social climate the practice of an adult couple inviting young children into their home, for a Bible lesson, would be viewed by many as sketchy. But this was the 1970s. Before cell phones, in our blue-collar Chicagoland neighborhood, kids ran together in packs and their parents rarely knew exactly where their kids were. They couldn't text or phone them to come home for dinner, so they opened the front door and yelled their kids' names in every direction to signal it was dinnertime. Helicopter parenting was not yet a thing, and many of the neighborhood parents trusted my parents *because* they were Christians. Being a church-going Christian was respected considerably more than it is now.

My mom and dad equipped themselves with the latest technology to communicate the timeless truths of the Bible to the youth of America. They used flannelgraphs (Google it) and flip charts to tell the stories of Jesus' miracles and the sacrifices of Hudson Taylor, the nineteenth century British missionary who founded the China Inland Mission and spent fifty-one years bringing the gospel to mainland China.

While my parents' teaching methods may seem archaic to you and me, they were quite effective in producing life-changing results in the lives of the children they taught. Many of the kids that came to our home for cookies and juice on Monday had prayed the sinner's prayer and committed their lives to Jesus by Friday.

Whether it was the power of the flannelgraph, the passion with which my parents told the stories, or the relentless pursuit of Jesus--the effect was powerful. I committed my life to Jesus after learning I would go to hell if I died without doing so. I prayed that prayer in faith as much as I did out of fear, the fear of being left out (FOBLO), something that would plague me the rest of my life.

When people hear about the path my life took in the years after this prayer, they often ask if my five-year-old faith was real. Did it take? I believe it did. I believe it because my heart was sincere about following Jesus. There was definitely a point where I let go of Jesus, but he never let go of me. Thankfully, much of my time and energy centered around Jesus in the years following that prayer, thanks in large part to my mother and grandfather who nurtured my faith and reinforced the biblical truths they taught me. In fact, my faith took on genuine meaning and purpose as we headed for the mission field in Copenhagen.

When we arrived in Denmark, my parents began calling me by my middle name, Erick, which would stick until I decided to go back to the name Todd in college. The Danes could not pronounce Todd as a name. The way they pronounced it sounded like a Danish word that refers to having disheveled hair. Erick, however, was a solid Scandinavian name.

Some of my most vivid childhood memories are of life in Copenhagen, Denmark, the homeland of my paternal grandfather. Copenhagen was urban, fast-paced and fun.

Every day seemed to bring a new discovery--The Little Mermaid statue in the harbor, Frederiksborg Castle, and Tivoli Gardens. I eagerly looked forward to Friday nights when we would walk from the parsonage we lived in (originally intended to be the home of the pastor of the Nazarene Church it was attached to) to the world-famous Tivoli Gardens, a must-see in Copenhagen. It is as brilliant as it is beautiful. Equal parts city gardens, amusement park, cultural center and concert venue, it featured buildings resembling those you would find in India, China and throughout Europe. When Tivoli lit up at night, it felt like the magical and wondrous center of the universe to my wide-eyed little self.

My grandparents were both Danish, which was the language often spoken in their home. Gram and Gramps must have used it when they didn't want my mother and my uncle to know what they were saying, because my mother landed in Denmark not knowing how to speak a lick of Danish. This meant that my parents would have to attend language school for the first few months we were in Copenhagen.

The only Danish I knew was the prayer my grandfather taught me to say before meals. That served as a nice icebreaker with the Danes--but not many people in Denmark were praying before their meals. My parents enrolled me in my own version of language school, which happened to be the full-day kindergarten across the street from our house. This was language immersion before language immersion was even a thing. It did not take me long to become fluent enough in Danish to serve as my parent's translator at restaurants and grocery stores around town.

Awkward

We had a very friendly albeit "European Hippie" family living in the house next door. Their only child, Greta, happened to be the only other child my age on the block; we quickly became best friends. Like many Danes, Greta's family members were far more progressive than Americans when it came to most things, including clothing--or no clothing for that matter. I came to believe that clothing in Denmark--whether at the park, the beach or at home--was optional. Greta's mother and father were not at all interested in knowing or following Jesus, but they loved having conservative American missionaries as their next-door neighbors. They seemed to revel in taking every opportunity they had to flaunt their very European lifestyle in the faces of my parents– which caused my mom and dad to feel quite uncomfortable and behave awkwardly around Greta's mother and father. Greta's mom owned and operated a small two-seat hair salon out of their remodeled foyer. She would often shampoo, cut, color and style her customer's hair while topless--as if it were nothing at all. My mother, desiring to be a good Christian woman, wrestled profoundly with whether to let me go to Greta's house. They were nudists! What else might be happening in that house? She was afraid that so much skin would have a negative impact on my young and developing psyche. It did not help my poor mother that I was all in when it came to being Danish. She was worried I would go so far as to adopt the "clothing optional" world view of Greta's family, which of course I did. It wasn't just Greta's family. All of Denmark and western Europe were parading around in their birthday suits when my mother would have preferred them to wear their swimsuits. Whether we were at the beach, the park, or the back yard--naked was often the way we were. With all this nakedness, my parents were careful not to include any pictures that showed me "living as the locals" in the slide shows they sent to the good folks from The Moody Church in Chicago who were supporting them financially.

My mother, bless her Scandinavian heart, got over the whole "going naked" thing when Greta's father knocked on the door one Sunday afternoon looking to borrow some sugar wearing only the measuring cup he held in his left hand. Mom tried to play it cool, but she was flustered and flabbergasted, which was the very reaction Greta's father was hoping to elicit from her. I'm sure that somewhere in Denmark, Greta's father still tells the story of shocking the American missionaries by "going commando with a measuring cup" at every dinner party he has attended since that Sunday afternoon he popped over to my parents' house looking for some sugar.

Denmark was very much a post-Christian country when we arrived. Thirty years after being liberated from Nazi German occupation, the Danish people had rebuilt their cities and their lives. God and religion had largely been swept away with the rubble of the past, but that didn't keep me from playing the dutiful role of mini-evangelist and neighborhood PR director for my parents' ministry. It was a role I cherished. Because my faith was both passionate and authentic, I believed that Jesus was always close by me. My young mind viewed Jesus more like an invisible friend and guardian angel than God. But I knew his story and believed that he was who my Bible said he was. He lived a sinless and blameless life; angered the religiously elite by hanging out with prostitutes and corrupt tax collectors. He was ultimately traded like a baseball card for a murderer called Barabbas and crucified as a substitutionary sacrifice for the sins of the world. While I didn't understand what substitutionary meant, I still believed Jesus died for me.

The kids in my neighborhood, including Greta, did not understand why Jesus mattered so much to me. I remember them asking me if Jesus was a ghost. "No," I said. "But he is right here with us--you just can't see him."

I vividly remember one of the older kids, Torbin, who would later become a close friend, throwing violent punches at the air around me hoping to land an uppercut to Jesus' jaw. He was violently opposed to Jesus. "I don't want him anywhere near me," he said in Danish.

I was heartbroken. I felt as though Torbin's attack on Jesus was an attack on me. How could Torbin hate Jesus?

Not long after that, I was invited to spend the night at Torbin's house. After a great day of hanging out, we were talking in his room as we were about to fall asleep. I don't remember exactly what I said, but I do remember talking about faith and Jesus to the point that it really upset him. Torbin told me to stop talking about God a few times before he stood up and said, "Stop talking about him or I'm going to kill you!"

We were kids; we often used hyperbole to make our point. Of course, I didn't really think Torbin wanted to kill me. When I responded that Jesus still loved him even though he had said he wanted to kill me, I knew I may have been pushing it a bit. Torbin lost it. In a rage, he jumped to his feet and pulled a razor-sharp dagger (which had no business being in the room of an eight-year-old boy) off the shelf above his bed. He stood over me on the bed in a terrifyingly intimidating way, with the dagger held above his head as though he was set to plunge it through my heart. At that point, I thought he may actually be serious about killing me. I was done talking about Jesus and I was done with our sleepover. I ran from his room, woke up his father and, without telling him what his son had done, asked him to walk me home. To this very day, as I write these words, I am convinced that Torbin was seriously thinking about killing me for talking about Jesus. I believe that because of what happened in subsequent days.

Two days after the dagger incident, Torbin came to our house for Five-Day Club. I told my parents what happened two nights before, but they didn't appear to take Torbin's threat to murder me very seriously. They seemed to be more committed to seeing Torbin come to faith, so they welcomed him back into our home. On this particular day, it was my mother who was talking with Torbin about Jesus. I don't remember what she said to him, but when she stopped talking, he blurted out, "Please come into my life so I can say your name…" After a few seconds he blurted out: "Jesus" as though the name had been stuck in his throat. Years later my mother would tell me that prior to that day, Torbin had been a somber kid with a certain darkness about him. She said that despite what I thought I remembered about Torbin, he had not said, nor been able to say, the name "Jesus" before his prayer for Jesus to save him. Whether Torbin could say the name of Jesus or not prior to his confession of faith, I don't know for sure. What's important to me is that I heard him make that confession of faith, and that he never pulled that stinking knife on me again!

It was in Copenhagen that I have my earliest memories of feeling insecure, alone and afraid as I listened to my parents scream at each other, slam doors and break dishes against the wall. Their marital drama fell into a rhythm that was almost predictable. However, that predictability didn't make it any less frightening or easier for me to deal with. They put on a good face for church people and the kids at our Five-Day Clubs, but they could only hide it for so long. The fighting took on a cadence that would only come to an end when my dad left the house, and my mother was in tears.

It wasn't as if my dad took a walk around the block or a drive around town to cool down. When he left, he was gone for what seemed like forever. Even years later, when he laid all his cards on the table about the secret life he lived while married to my mother, he never told me where he went.

We left Copenhagen after just three years. I didn't know it then, but we had to leave Denmark because my parent's marriage was rapidly disintegrating to the point that it was no longer healthy for them to be on the mission field.

ANCHOR IN THE WIND

My parents' marriage was headed toward the rocks, but we landed on our feet back in Chicago. Initially, we took up residence in the semi-finished basement of my grandparents' three-bedroom, two-bathroom brick bungalow on 157th Street. Their house looked exactly like every other house on the block and like half the rows upon rows of bungalows throughout Chicago. We lived in a tiny room in the far corner of the basement, which, if there had been a closet, would have counted as a bedroom. It wasn't a great space for a family of four, but it worked for us.

I loved living in that house because it gave me a chance to see my grandparents every day. This was especially sweet because my grandmother, who battled diabetes and had both legs amputated, would die just over a year after we returned to Chicago.

My grandfather came to the Christian faith shortly after arriving in America as a nineteen-year-old Danish immigrant. His faith, his family, and his country were the three most important things in his life--followed closely by his 1976 canary yellow Buick LeSabre with a white canopy, which he kept freshly waxed and covered in his detached garage. I was his first grandchild. As such, he kept me close, spoiled me a little and made absolutely certain to impress the value of regular church attendance on my young heart. He was a short man with an understated personality, a thick Danish accent and a laugh so infectious that once he started laughing everyone around him would soon be laughing-- even if they weren't quite sure what they were laughing about. I loved him deeply and believed he would always be there for me. I'm sad that I only knew him as an older man. He was sixty-five years old when I was born, which didn't give us much time together. However, now that I think about it, we would eventually have exactly the right amount of time together. More on that later.

Though my parents may have been strongly encouraged to return to Chicago from Denmark, I don't think the missionary agency ever invested any time or energy in helping my parents strengthen their marriage. I do know that they were kept on the payroll and that my dad was reassigned to other ministry roles in Chicago.

He was asked to lead an outreach ministry called Dial-a-Story. The name says all you need to know. Moody Church kids were given tiny key chain phones to share with all their friends at school and in their neighborhoods. When a child called the number on the phone, they heard a short, pre-recorded Bible story. If the caller had not yet "asked Jesus into their heart," they were encouraged to stay on the line to talk with an adult who would walk them through the process and/or pray with them for any specific needs they may have had. Dial-a-Story was certainly an idea for its time. Inviting children to call a phone number and end up speaking to a strange adult, in today's world, would face all kinds of obstacles and would likely not pass the creeper test. Still, Dial-a-Story had such a great run under my dad's leadership that he ended up on Channel 38, Chicago's Christian television station, talking about the impact it was having on the lives of children throughout the city. I'll never forget the ugly green suit he wore on-air—so embarrassing.

As a city kid, I loved attending Moody Church. Its location on the Near North Side of Chicago just across the street from Lincoln Park made it an urban paradise for my friends and me. In the late 1970s and early 1980s, our parents were not very concerned about knowing where we were every moment of the day--not the way I am with my three daughters. I would regularly meet my friends, Junior, Lenny and Danny after Sunday School to decide what our agenda was for the next ninety minutes, while our parents were in the church service. It's ironic that Warren Wiersbe, who pastored the church back then, is one of my favorite theologians to quote when I preach. I only ever heard him preach if I was being punished and made to sit through a service rather than hang with my friends.

Moody was a culturally and socio-economically diverse church. Lenny was born in Mexico and lived with his mother in a North side high-rise with an awesome view of the city. Junior was from a large Filipino family and lived in one of Chicago's Filipino neighborhoods. My family lived in an all-white blue-collar neighborhood on the South side, and Danny, whose family was extremely wealthy, lived in one of the well-manicured old money homes near Lake Michigan, just North of the city where the city parks had grass tennis courts like you'd find at the All-England Club at Wimbledon. Our circle of friends included Latinos and Latinas, Jamaicans and African Americans. We spent much of our childhood weekends and Wednesday nights playing hide and seek inside the old Moody Church--which had a massive auditorium, many nooks and crannies, and a labyrinth of a basement that was perfect for the game. When we became bored inside the building, we would cross the street and play in the park, sit on the steps of the Chicago Historical Society, or simply hit the mini-mart at the gas station on LaSalle Street.

I recently took my family to see Moody Church. When I told my daughters that their grandparents used to let me run around the neighborhood when I was younger than they were, Sophie, who was thirteen, asked me if my parents loved me. "If they loved you, why would they let you roam the streets of Chicago?" she wondered.

It was a different time.

While my dad was having success at Dial-a-Story, it was clear that his heart was not in it. In fact, it was becoming increasingly difficult for him to present the façade that everything in his life was fine and that we were just another happy, well-adjusted Christian family. While none of us saw it at the time, my father was battling inner demons that had plagued him since his traumatic childhood in Wakefield, Michigan. Wakefield was a small blue-collar town where everyone seemed to work in either the timber industry or the iron ore mines. Yet, there were many who were barely getting by and forced to collect welfare checks. My dad's parents were raging alcoholics and horrific parents who had each found a way to abandon my dad and his brother in their own unique way. My grandfather simply left them to pursue the bottle and, seemingly, any woman who would have him in her bed. My grandmother drank herself to death, dying tragically of a massive stroke at the age of thirty-two. My dad witnessed the entire thing when he was only thirteen years old.

My dad and his younger brother Don bounced around from one relative to another before landing at their Uncle Ole and Aunt Jen's home. My father's saving grace was the relationship he forged with his four female cousins, two of whom were gay but unable to come out in a culture that would have annihilated and ostracized them if they had. As kids they all had to become survivors who looked out for and protected each other--especially during the alcoholic rages of Aunt Jen who would get black-out drunk and chase her husband around their home with a shotgun. I only knew Jen and Ole long after they gave up drinking as tender, loving, salt-of-the-earth people. My mother often used their example of love and selflessness as non-Christians to put some of the Christians she knew to shame. She wasn't altogether wrong.

I don't know how much of my dad's upbringing contributed to the secret he carried or the double life he lived those many years, but he certainly didn't have a puncher's chance of being a stable husband or father. Going to Moody Bible Institute, pursuing a life in ministry, marrying the first girl who took an interest in him, and starting a family with her had not quieted his demons. He could not continue to fake as much as he was and hope to keep it all together. To let some of the pressure out of his life, he resigned from Dial-a-Story, got out of ministry, and took a corporate job on Michigan Avenue in the heart of Chicago's Magnificent Mile.

My dad may have had his demons, but he was quite impressive, very smart, and highly motivated. He took a job at the Oil-Dri corporation at 520 North Michigan Avenue, a company that made industrial strength oil absorbents and

Cat's Pride Cat Litter. The role my dad was offered was essentially that of a glorified secretary. They titled it differently to allow a man to still feel masculine--but he was a secretary. He spent a few months in that job before he was promoted. Within a few years, my father, who possessed only an associate degree in Bible from Moody Bible Institute, became the vice president of purchasing.

We moved to a nicer home in a better neighborhood. My dad stopped going to church and started traveling a lot to Georgia and Florida on business, all while my parents' marriage continued to unravel. My mother, bless her soul, was committed to keeping faith in the fabric of our family, which was not an easy task. My sisters and I made sure of that. We left Moody Church and started attending a church closer to home, Moraine Valley Community Church in Palos Heights, Illinois. There was a lot I loved about this church too, but my faith, though still alive, was quickly taking a backseat to other interests in my life like baseball, television shows, music and girls. I loved singing in the kids choir and quite often landed big roles in our all-city productions. I also loved going to AWANA, which, on the outside, looked a little like a Christian version of the Boy Scouts. In reality, only the shirts were similar. AWANA was all about memorizing Bible verses, a great way to get familiar with the Bible. The fact that ribbons and trophies were passed out for scripture memorization made it about the reward as much, if not more, than the Bible being memorized. But I can recall verses that I need for nearly any circumstance in my life because of what I memorized in AWANA.

The fact that my dad didn't go to church made it very difficult for my two younger sisters and me to want to go to church. Every Sunday morning my mother would wake us up and sometimes literally drag us to church. We were that family that complained, bickered, and argued all the way to church. When we arrived, my mother would look us each dead in the eye and say something like, "Now, you are going to go to your Sunday School class and you are going to smile and be happy about it!" By the time we saw our first fellow parishioner we were all smiling and playing the part my mother had threatened us to play.

My dad and I had a very close relationship when I was young. Every Saturday, when he was in town, we would have breakfast at the Golden Bear Restaurant on 159th Street. We often went to movies together and we regularly spent twenty or more nights at Comiskey Park cheering on the lowly Chicago White Sox. When my parents had fights, which seemed to be all the time, my dad would come and apologize to me for having to suffer in a family where my parents didn't love each other. He did more than apologize. He often shared details of their disagreements, from his perspective of course, which caused me to side with him and distrust my mother, something she did not deserve. It was pure manipulation on my dad's part. That form of manipulation would soon put me in the very undesirable and unfair position of knowing more about why my parents' marriage was failing than my mother knew about her own marriage, which had disastrous consequences.

My dad's boss was from Mississippi and hated living in Chicago. He was always on the lookout for a way to move the purchasing department to a Southern location. It made a lot of financial and practical sense as much of the purchasing my dad's team did was from companies in Southern Georgia and North Florida--places my dad was already spending a lot of time.

I was over-the-moon thrilled when my dad invited me to join him on a business trip to Florida and Georgia as a twelfth birthday present. I had never been to that part of the country. Once there, I quickly determined that it was nothing like Chicago and that they did not always treat people from the North with the Southern charm and hospitality one might expect. We spent the first few nights in a Days Inn just outside Thomasville, Georgia. My dad was at the plant all day, leaving me alone at the hotel with not much to do. I decided to leave the hotel room and take a walk to explore a little bit of Thomasville--but I left my key in the hotel room. When I went to the front desk to tell the gentleman that I had locked myself out and needed a new key, he asked me for identification. I was twelve. I didn't even have a library card. I gave him my name, my father's name and I described the contents of the room. Not only did I do all of that, but it was also abundantly clear by my accent that I was not a native of Southern Georgia. My accent was the primary reason he left me sitting outside the hotel room for several hours until my father returned. He said he couldn't let me in without verifying my identity. The truth was I was a Yankee; there was no way he was going to help *me*--even if I was just a kid. He could have offered me some basic human kindness, but he chose not to. He never offered to call my parents, nor did he allow me to use a house phone to call them myself.

Instead, he pointed me to a pay phone over a mile away where I could make a collect call to my mother. When my dad returned to the hotel and heard the story, he was livid. But that's just the way it was in Thomasville, Georgia. The hotel manager was unsympathetic and there was nothing but a feigned apology offered to make amends.

That was my first taste of life in the South. I have since come to know that ninety-nine percent of Southerners would have helped me that day. The unfriendly man working the Days Inn counter was one of those who still seemed angry enough about having lost the Civil War that he was willing to take it out on a twelve-year-old kid. Simply because I was from Chicago.

Three months later, my dad announced to my family that we were moving to Tallahassee, Florida. Just thirty miles south of my fond memories and old friend at the Thomasville Days Inn. I was not ready for the tsunami of culture shock, and ensuing devastation, that move would have on me and my family.

TASTE OF PREJUDICE

Moving to Tallahassee, Florida was a lot like going to a foreign country. Before arriving there, I had no idea that Florida had two cultures: coastal culture and, with rare exception, everything else. Coastal culture is all about the beach, major cities, the Atlantic Ocean to the east and the white sands of the Gulf Coast to the west. Tallahassee fell into the "everything else" category, even though it was a major college town and the state capital. It's technically Florida, but it felt very much like extra-Southern Georgia to me.

We arrived in Tallahassee in August, just before my eighth-grade year. Making a move of this magnitude during adolescence proved to be quite traumatic for me. For example, it was shocking to see that, just outside of town, multi-generational African American families were living in dilapidated shacks with no air conditioning or indoor plumbing. It was an astonishing sight you might have expected to see in 1883 but not in 1983. Having lived in large cities in the U.S. and Europe, I didn't realize there were still places in America where families were using outhouses and living in such regrettable circumstances. It was other-worldly.

On my first day as a student at Cobb Middle School, I was caught off guard when one of the neighborhood kids came to the bus stop and declared, "I just want y'all to know that in case any (N-word) come, I'm sittin' in the back of the bus."

I was shocked, not only by what he said, but at the laugh he got from the bus stop crowd. Back in Chicago, two of my best friends and bandmates were African American, they would have gone to blows with anyone reckless enough to make a comment like that. At the bus stop that day, I began to realize that black kids and white kids were not really friends, and they definitely didn't hang out together. This was one-hundred and twenty years after slavery was abolished and decades after segregation had officially ended in the South.

The prejudice of the racist kid at the bus stop knew no bounds. He turned his attention to a mom and her two sons waiting on the bus in their station wagon. When he saw that their car had New York license plates, he said, "Look at that, y'all. *Yankees*! You can't get more Yankee than to be a New York Yankee." This kid wasn't exactly Mensa material, but, unfortunately, he gave me my first taste of what life in Tallahassee would be like.

Anthony and Joey Vinti were in that station wagon. They were twin brothers from New York City who had recently moved to Florida because their father, Big Joe Vinti, had just retired from a thirty-year career with the NYPD. The reason their mom drove them to the bus stop was that Joey had Cerebral Palsy. The disease had a crippling effect on Joey's body, motor skills and speech. He could walk, but CP had contorted his body so badly that it was difficult for him to get very far. But Joey was a tough kid, New York City tough. He didn't want any pity, he rarely sat out when the neighborhood kids were playing sports, and he would get out-of-his-mind enraged if we even hinted at taking it easy on him. He may have been from New York, but he and his Yankee family had more character, integrity and heart than the joker at the bus stop. I don't remember the joker's name, but I'll never forget the Vinti family.

Prior to moving to Florida, I had been the first trumpet, second chair, in a band made up of kids from three large Chicago area schools. This did not at all impress Mr. Miller, the Cobb Middle School band teacher, who seemed to judge me instantly simply because I was from Chicago, which made me a Yankee in his eyes too.

"Where you from, boy?" Miller asked with a slow Southern drawl.

I had never been referred to by an adult, or anyone else for that matter, as "boy." It didn't feel good. It wasn't intended to.

"Chicago," I replied feeling slightly intimidated. "I was first trumpet, second chair."

"I figured as much," he snarked. "Well, let's see if you can play. Let me hear it, son!"

After giving what I thought was a respectable enough solo performance, Mr. Miller sent me to the third trumpet section, band purgatory. That was the moment I lost all interest in playing the trumpet. Mr. Miller had patronized and embarrassed me, which was all it took to devote myself to disrupting Mr. Miller's fourth period band class. I was unafraid of what the consequences might be.

In the third trumpet section, I sat next to a tall blonde-haired kid with the perfect name, Shane. Shane wore a t-shirt with a skull sporting a black cowboy hat with the rebel flag flying in the background. He pointed to the letters CSA, which were featured prominently on the skull's cowboy hat, and declared with great enthusiasm, "You see this? The Confederate States of America. The South is going to rise again!"

When I got home later that day, I went straight to my dad and asked, "Where in the *hell* did you move us to? What is wrong with these people?" His response was to reprimand me for swearing and tell me to "Suck it up."

In Mr. Miller's band you only got one warning for being disruptive in class. After that, he wrote your name on the blackboard--indicating you were on thin ice and would have to write a paper apologizing for your behavior. If you earned a single check next to your name, you were going to detention. If you got two checks by your name, it was all of the above plus a phone call home and, with parental blessing, a swat to the butt with the mini canoe paddle Mr. Miller kept in his office. Spankings for thirteen-year-old eighth-graders!

We were just a few weeks into the school year when I committed myself to hitting Mr. Miller's classroom discipline trifecta. I practically begged Mr. Miller to call my parents that day.

A few minutes into the period, I was talking when I should have been playing my trumpet. Mr. Miller barely missed a beat as he turned and wrote my name on the chalkboard. He skipped the verbal warning! In protest, I promptly got up from my seat, went to the front of the class, picked up an eraser, and removed my name from the chalkboard. The class was instantly abuzz. "That's the Yankee kid from Chicago!" they said. "He's fixin' to get the paddle, y'all!"

I was fixin' to get something, but I was so angry that I did not care. I was angry at how Mr. Miller treated me and I was livid that my parents moved me from Chicago to a place where people were as openly and casually racist as they were bitter at having lost the Civil War. Mr. Miller rewrote my name on the board and promptly put a check next to it. Detention. Not a problem.

I decided to tap into my creative side and draw a bow-legged cowboy caricature of Mr. Miller wearing a CSA hat and shooting the middle finger from the hip with both hands. My fellow band mates around me loved it as it was quite the likeness. Their laughter, however, sold me out. "Morrison!" Miller yelled. "Boy, you best bring whatever is so gosh darn funny down here right this instant!"

I will admit to feeling like I had taken things a little too far. I quickly attempted to erase the double "birds," but I couldn't get the job done before Mr. Miller was standing over me.

He looked at the picture and asked, "Is this me, son?" What was I going to say?

"Yep. That's you," I confessed.

"Yes, *what!*?!?" he demanded.

I didn't realize that he was expecting me to say "Yes, Sir," like the local kids did. Back in Chicago, if you called somebody a sir, you might get your butt kicked for being a wise acre.

"This looks like me shootin' the bird," he said, with dismay.

"Noooo," I said, as I searched for a plausible alternative. "It's you . . . uh . . . holding pistols."

The students around us busted out in laughter at my brash disregard for his authority, which only served to escalate the situation.

"Go get your momma on the phone right now!" he said angrily, but with a winning smirk on his face, as he pointed me toward the telephone in his office.

I was more than happy to call my mother and tell her what a backwater hick of a redneck my band teacher was. My mom was not too pleased at the reason she was hearing from me. Fortunately, she had not exactly been feeling the warmth of Southern Hospitality herself since our arrival in Tallahassee. As a result, there was less than a snowball's chance she was going to let old Mr. Miller take a swat at her son with his canoe paddle. She told him that she and my father would handle the discipline themselves. When I arrived home that day, my mom was waiting for me with a huge bowl of ice cream. Victory for the Yankee from Chicago!

I struggled mightily in Tallahassee. I missed the friends and the culture we had left behind in Chicago. I was a lonely kid who had a hard time making new friends in Florida. I'm an extrovert, but anyone who met me in those days would never have believed it. I connected with other kids like me who were not from the South. I hung out with Anthony and Joey Viniti and a surfer kid from Long Beach, California who found a way to insert the word "dude" into nearly every sentence. I could not find my bearings; I was lonely, angry, and probably severely depressed. I didn't know how to deal with any of it, so I lashed out at those closest to me--my family. I lashed out because I felt betrayed by the move from Chicago and because I expected Florida to be fun--you know, beaches, palm trees, and Disney World. I lashed out because my parents' marriage was disintegrating, as was the foundation my family had always been for me. My dad and I were no longer getting breakfast on Saturday mornings or going to the movies together as we had done so often back home in Chicago. There were only college teams in Tallahassee and football was king. The nearest Major League Baseball game was a few hundred miles away in Atlanta.

DUELING IDENTITIES

I began to question if business was really the reason my dad was gone from home as much as he was when Alan, a sheriff from a county somewhere in Southern Georgia, began leaving curious messages on our home answering machine. He would often call just after my dad returned home from what I believed had been a business trip to make sure he got home safely. Who was this guy and why did he care so much about when or how my dad got home? It got even stranger when my dad showed me a picture he kept of Alan, in full uniform, standing alongside his police cruiser. My dad attempted to reassure me that the relationship was on the level by saying, "He's just a friend I met, at a bar. He really cares about me, that's all it is."

The affectionate longing in both their voices was anything but reassuring. I did not understand that relationship and it was beyond strange that my dad carried Alan's picture around in his briefcase. The whole nature of the relationship was troubling, and I was so afraid that it actually *was* what it looked like that I pushed the truth aside in favor of my preferred reality--that they were just friends.

The Big Reveal

I was thrilled when my dad surprised me with a weekend trip to Atlanta to see the Braves play the Chicago Cubs. It meant the world to me that my dad may have noticed how difficult adjusting to life in the South had been for me. A trip like this was exactly what we needed to reconnect and rediscover our relationship.

We landed in Atlanta mid-morning on Friday and immediately checked into the Peachtree Plaza Hotel. I could see the ballpark from our hotel room and could not wait to get there. We hung out downtown most of the day, took in the sights, and ran into several people from Chicago who were also there to see the Cubs. The first game was epic. It was 1984, the first time in decades the Cubs would make it to the post-season. Ryne Sandberg, Gary Matthews and "The Penguin," Ron Cey, all hit bombs to lead the Cubs to victory. That night we dined on swordfish and filet mignon, celebrating victory in the rotating restaurant atop the hotel. I remember thinking this was the best time I'd had with my dad in a very long time.

Saturday started as a gloriously sunny day full of promise for me and for the Cubs. My dad was eager to take me to breakfast at a place he said he visited every time he came to Atlanta. Our hotel was on the South end of downtown and the restaurant he took me to was on the North end of the city--a long way to go for a decent omelet. Just as we took our seats, we were greeted by a boisterous waiter in his twenties who was very excited to see us. The first thing he said in an enthusiastic Southern accent was, "Hey, Al! It's so good to see you, Sweetie. Who is this fine young man you've brought with you, today?" The next thing I knew my dad was introducing me to his friend, Dwayne. Several questions ran through my mind. "How does my dad know Dwayne? Is Dwayne gay? Yes, he must be. Why did he call my dad, 'Sweetie'?" I quickly tried to rationalize that my dad only knew Dwayne because he had eaten breakfast there before and Dwayne had obviously been his server. Plus,

Dwayne was a flaming extrovert, he probably spoke this way to all his customers. I nearly had myself convinced. But something wasn't right. The banter between my dad and Dwayne was all too familiar, it revealed a deeper history between them.

After breakfast, we drove through what my memory sees as Atlanta's version of the Castro district in San Francisco. It was clearly a predominantly gay neighborhood. We turned onto a street with a park on one side and a row of affluent homes on the other. When we came to a line of cars parked on the right side of the street my dad slowed the car to a snail's pace, I noticed that there were men, who appeared to be waiting for someone, in the driver seat of each car in the line. I had no idea they were waiting for me.

When we reached a newer model Mercedes, the driver side door propped open slightly to reveal the man in the driver's seat was wearing a trench coat. When he and I were face-to-face he opened that trench coat to reveal he was wearing nothing underneath. When he saw that he was flashing a fourteen-year-old kid, he quickly covered himself and shut the car door.

I was shocked, at a loss for words, and increasingly wounded by the day's events. It was barely noon; what would the rest of the day bring?

I desperately wanted to tell my dad how confused, hurt and afraid I was, but I could not find the words, or the resolve, to confront him.

My dad seemed slightly shocked himself by the flasher in the Mercedes. He tried to laugh it off by saying, "Did that guy just flash us?" No, he flashed *me*, and I will never be able to unsee that image or forget it. I still remember the detail and surprise in the flasher's face, more than thirty-five years later.

A sadness I had never felt before, but have experienced many times since, washed over me that day. There were things I did not know about my dad. He had been keeping secrets from his family. These weren't small things like smoking cigarettes when he was away from home. He did that too. But, in light of all that he revealed that day, the smoking didn't even register.

My dad had not taken me to Atlanta to reconnect with me--or to see the Cubs. He had taken me there to show me his "spots" and introduce me to his "friends." My dad was showing me what he was apparently too afraid to tell me. He was gay.

I didn't want to believe it, but my denial didn't make it less true. A severe burden engulfed my soul. I couldn't identify it then because I was too young to put it together. I had learned things about my dad: his "business trips," Sheriff Alan, Dwayne, and the trench coat in the Mercedes, that no one else knew. I knew why my mother's marriage to my father could never work. She did not. Holding that secret would prove to be too much for me.

I don't remember going to the Cubs game that night, but I think we were there. I do remember my dad leaving me alone in the hotel room and not returning until nearly 3 a.m. I remember the profound sense of dread I had the next morning about returning to Tallahassee. What would I say to my mother and my sisters with all I had just discovered and experienced? Would I say anything at all? Doing the right thing would have disastrous consequences for everyone in my family. It would certainly blow my family up, instantaneously. The power contained in my new-found discovery about my father's secret life was overwhelming. I felt paralyzed by fear, guilt, and dread.

My dad was too hung over to get up in time for the 1 p.m. game on Sunday. He gave me a wad of cash and told me to ask the doorman in the lobby for a cab to the ballpark. I sat roughly twenty rows behind the Braves dugout; but the game that played out before me was nothing more than a blur. Baseball was just one of the many things that no longer mattered in light of my new reality. My life would never be the same. My family would never be the same. I could sense the impending doom as everything I held dear was about to come crashing down around me.

POWERFUL ALLIES

I have often wondered whether my father felt a sense of relief after that trip to Atlanta. He was no longer carrying his secret alone--he had placed it squarely on the shoulders of his fourteen-year-old son who had no idea what to do with it. Had it made him feel better to introduce me to Dwayne and take me cruising? Did he somehow think he had done a good thing? Was this really his way of coming out to me? I have no idea what his intentions were, nor do I have any idea how all of this had made him feel. I can tell you without any doubt that he had no idea what the events of that day did to me.

The whole thing was so terribly dysfunctional, uncaring, and selfish. Why couldn't he have used that weekend to sit down with me, look me in the eye, and do his very best to tell his truth? He did not tell me anything. Instead, he showed me he was gay--in the creepiest way possible. I will never know if he felt relief after that trip or not. I am, however, confident that he had no idea what he did to my young heart; my sense of security, and to my ability to trust. The weight of knowing what my mother and two younger sisters did not yet know was as crushing as it was unfair. It was impossible for my fourteen-year-old self to hold his secret and function as though everything was fine. I isolated and alienated myself from those I loved as I descended into a deep depression and destructive rage.

Soon after that involuntary fact-finding trip to Atlanta, I traveled to Chicago to spend the summer with extended family and friends. While it was great to be "home" and away from the pressure-cooker environment my dad had created for my family, I could not get out from under the weight of what I had experienced in Atlanta. I confided in my most trusted friends at the time, Becky and Joy. At that age, my guy friends were of no help to me. They could not hear that my dad was gay without behaving awkwardly and making insensitive jokes. It was unfair of me to dump my emotional garbage on Becky and Joy, who were completely ill-equipped to step into the madness of my life. Yet, they were true friends who chose to sit with me in my pain, which was exactly what I needed and so good for my soul. Both Becky and Joy insisted I stay with their families while I was in Chicago. Their parents had known me for many years and were concerned enough about me to open their homes to me. I am forever grateful to the Winship and Brown families for taking me in that summer. They played a big role in rescuing me by making me believe that, regardless of what had happened, or was happening, in my life, I was not alone in this world. There were people who loved me and would be there for me no matter what. Those families left an imprint of selfless grace on my heart that will stay with me forever.

*****

I was recently in St Louis, where I officiated the funeral of a lifelong friend, Shaun, who took his life after a long and painful battle with PTSD. In the months preceding his death, I did my best to give Shaun a reason to live as we talked about how valuable his life was to his children, his family--and to me. He was a two-tour veteran of the war in Iraq and had done multiple tours in Korea. He flew in Blackhawk helicopters and experienced the full scope of war and all its horrors. I had known Shaun since we were both nine years old. We experienced so much together growing up just outside of Chicago and Shaun had influenced my life in so many ways. I can say, without hesitation, that if he had not been my friend when I was 18, I don't know where I'd be right now. I loved Shaun. He was in my wedding and I was in his wedding. We were true friends. He died in August of 2020. When we spoke in late July, I was confident we would see each other soon. We were making plans to use my frequent flyer miles for him to come to Seattle. I ended up using those miles to travel to St. Louis for his funeral.

One of the sweet surprises that tragedy sometimes offers is that it reunites people who have drifted apart on the waves of circumstance and time. I did not expect to run into Gene and Chris Winship at Shaun's memorial. I had not seen them in more than 30 years. When I reintroduced myself to them, they were as thrilled to see me as I was to see them. It filled my heart to tell them that taking me in all those years ago had kept me afloat at a time I desperately needed someone to throw me a lifeline. I will never forget, and will always be thankful for, the love they showed me. It was a beautiful reunion and great gift to all three of us on an otherwise tragic occasion.

*****

Both Joy and Becky were mature beyond their years and wise enough to refer me to someone who could offer me real help. Becky made some phone calls and set up a meeting with someone much more equipped to counsel and guide me through the minefield of my life, Marian Johnson.

Marian Johnson was a sweet woman, one of the sweetest I have known. She was also one of the strongest women I knew as a child--which is why I loved her. Marian was the wife of the pastor of Moraine Valley Community Church, where my family and I had been heavily involved before moving to Tallahassee. Pastor Bill and Marian had been friends of my parents, which meant they knew my situation quite well. I will never forget sitting in their sunken family room in Palos Heights, telling Marian, or Mrs. Johnson as I called her then, what I had seen and experienced in Atlanta. Bill and Marian Johnson were the least Baptist Baptists I may have ever encountered. I told an honest version of events--complete with my own R-rated commentary about what I had seen. I'm not sure how many f-bombs I may have dropped, but Marian never flinched. She did the very thing I needed her to do, she hugged me and told me I was loved, that I mattered deeply to a lot of people, and that I always had a place to belong. I believed her. But I would still have to return to Tallahassee--where I would have to face the fate of my family without the support of my people--who were all in Chicago.

Marian Johnson died several years ago, but she remained in touch with me until the end of her life. She was the truest of true friends and I am forever thankful for the role she and Pastor Bill played in my life. Without them, my life would certainly have taken a different path.

Though I hardly saw them, my mother and sisters had also been in Chicago that summer. Because things between us were so tense, my mother was quite happy to let me do my thing while she and my sisters did their thing. When we returned to Tallahassee, just before school was set to begin, we were shocked to see that my dad was not the same person we had left behind just two months earlier. He had lost what appeared to be thirty pounds, dyed his hair from graying-brown to blonde, revamped his wardrobe, and purchased a sports car. This was a midlife crisis on steroids, though my dad was only thirty-six years old. By the time school started, my parents had split, my dad "came out" a little more, found a new "friend," and moved closer to living an openly gay life.

I could not fully appreciate it at the time, but the fact that my father had cheated on my mother was a devastating betrayal of their marriage covenant. The fact that he had cheated on her with other men was a whole different level of infidelity. A betrayal my mother would never get over; it would take her nearly twenty years to move past it. Remember, my parents had been conservative evangelical Christian missionaries. This was not how their life was supposed to go. A story like this is hardly surprising in today's world, but it was scandalous in the 1980s It absolutely devastated my mother--something I did not recognize or help her with. Instead of aligning with her and finding strength from one another, I blamed her for my pain and made her life exponentially more difficult than it needed to be.

I was in nine kinds of pain myself, over what was transpiring in my family. But I didn't possess the tools to put my finger on a single one of them. So, I lashed out and made life miserable for almost everyone around me. I lashed out at my teachers; I lashed out at Rob, the therapist my parents sent me to, and to my everlasting shame, I lashed out at my mother. She was reeling from the betrayal of a man none of us really knew, least of all her; and my greatest contribution to her in that season was that I intentionally made her life hell. I now know that much of how I treated her had to do with how much guilt I carried for knowing about my father's secrets and infidelities for months without telling her. His story may not have been mine to tell; but I knew I had betrayed my mother by not sharing what I knew.

I had once been so close to my father, but now I was barely a blip on his radar. I did not factor into his new life. He begrudgingly allowed me to move in with him because things between my mother and me were so volatile. Plus, it was September and school was about to begin. I needed a place to live. There were moments when he seemed to make an effort at being my dad. He took me shopping, bought me new clothes and had his hairdresser give me a great new look. I must admit that having a gay father does have some advantages. Style and fashion were a big deal for my dad. He did a *Queer Eye for the Straight Guy* makeover on me just before my sophomore year--*and it worked*. Prior to that, I had been invisible in high school. Now, I was a fashion statement with an angry edge who smelled sweetly of Polo by Ralph Lauren. The cute girls in my classes started asking *me* out! I loved it! Being noticed and pursued was a great diversion and the only good thing I had going for me. However, my newly discovered popularity at Lincoln High School would be short-lived. By mid-October I would be in a new school in a new town.

My dad quickly came to realize that he could not fully be himself and live the life he wanted to live with his teenage son living with him. He wanted to bring men home from the club to do whatever they wanted without worrying about what I would see or hear. Not only did I cramp his style, I was a constant reminder of the pain he was causing his family. He had to get rid of me.

FINAL ARRANGEMENT

The last thing my mother and father ever did together was agree to send me to Michigan, twelve hundred miles away from the chaos, to live with my dad's brother Don and family. Oh, by the way, not the "baking glove" part of Michigan you are thinking of, but the rural Upper Peninsula of Michigan--Wakefield to be specific, the town where my dad had grown up. It felt like Siberia, which made me feel even more isolated.

FOBLO (the fear of being left out) and the fear of rejection and abandonment linger within me to this day, because of my parents' decision to ship me off to be somebody else's problem.

The day my dad took me to the airport, I had every intention of leaving Tallahassee, but I had no intention of going to Michigan. I negotiated a weekend stopover in Chicago so I could see my grandfather and a few of my friends. My game plan was to convince any one of them, and their parents, to let me live with them. I spent a frantic weekend in Chicago going from place to place sharing my story and doing my best manipulation. But, to my great despair, no one was prepared to add an instant fifteen-year-old, with my baggage, to their situation. Why would they be?

I remember wondering how much my father paid my aunt and uncle to take me in. I was certain it must have been quite the carrot. They were very poor, often unemployed, and struggled to provide for their own three children. It had to be a difference-maker for them to be willing to add me to the mix under those circumstances.

I may have been left with no other option than to go to Michigan, but that did not mean I was going to make it easy on my parents. My flight from Chicago to Ironwood, Michigan had a connection in Minneapolis. I dreaded the idea of living in the "UP" (Upper Peninsula) with family members I had not seen in years and barely knew. I felt abandoned, unloved, vulnerable, and alone. I was terrified. It didn't help that my plane encountered the most violent wind shear I have ever experienced. If we had not hit it at more than twenty-thousand feet we would have crashed--it was that intense. I share that because that wind shear was the perfect metaphor for my life at the time; the turbulence was so violent and chaotic that I actually thought I might not survive. When I arrived at the Minneapolis airport, I made the decision that I was not going to Michigan that day.

I made that decision without a plan or more than $50 in my pocket. What I did have was an insatiable desire to make my parents feel some of the pain I was feeling over what they were doing to me. After missing the last connecting flight of the day to Ironwood, I called my parents and said, "You wanted to get rid of me? Fine. I'm in Minneapolis but I am not going to Michigan." I had so little control in my life. I couldn't control anything my parents did, I couldn't control being separated from my little sisters, and I couldn't control that no one in Chicago was willing to take me in--but I could control whether or not I would go to Michigan that day.

That was the moment I became a survivor. I would no longer let decisions by my parents, or anyone else, create consequences that simply happened *to* me. I would no longer be a victim of their choices. I wanted a say in what happened to me--even if it was detrimental to my physical, emotional, and spiritual health.

My parents could not do much about the fact that I was staying in Minneapolis from their homes in Florida. That was the point. They did convince me to talk with Rob, the counselor I had seen in Tallahassee. While I am a huge proponent of therapy and have been going to therapy for years, Rob didn't help me at all. I spoke to him because I hoped he might be an ally, but Rob was my mother's counselor, not mine. The only thing I remember Rob telling my fifteen-year-old self was that I was in a thick jungle and he was a jungle guide. He was the only one in the jungle with a machete big enough to cut a path out of that jungle. I love a good metaphor, but I didn't understand what the heck Rob was talking about.

Even if I got out of that jungle, my parents would still be divorced, my dad would still be gay, my parents had still decided to abandon me, and my family was still blown apart. Leaving the jungle was as terrifying to me as remaining in it; there were no good options. Of course, Rob's metaphor makes perfect sense to me now, but I needed something a little more helpful from him that day.

The fact that I was giving a huge middle finger to my parents and to Rob the counselor had my parents half-worried about my safety and half wishing they could kill me themselves. Regardless of how they felt about what I was doing, neither of them suggested I come home, nor did either of them come after me. That was extremely painful because, in my own highly defiant way, I was making a bid, if not a plea, for one of those two things. I wanted them to love me enough to come after me--or bring me home.

I did have all the power in this negotiation. So, I negotiated a flight back to Chicago so I could spend a few more days with family and friends while continuing the dialogue about whether I would go to Michigan. After three more days in Chicago nothing had really changed. The only place available for me to live was with Uncle Don and Aunt Bev in Wakefield.

What I put those poor people through was nothing less than agonizing. Don and Bev are truly salt-of-the-earth people. They were terrified something happened to me when I wasn't on the plane from Minneapolis. They felt more responsible for me than anyone else in my family. That was made abundantly clear to me when I learned they had not received any money from my dad. They took me in because they loved me. They still do.

PENINSULA LIVING

I will always remember the late afternoon October flight over Northwestern Wisconsin. I distinctly remember how the setting sun lit the forest ablaze with the orange, yellow and red colors of Fall. It was glorious, but I still associate the colors of Fall with the trauma I was feeling about being abandoned and shipped off by my family. Even now, for just a split second when I see the trees turn, the residual ache of the profound loneliness and sense of dread I felt that day washes over me. It is probably a good thing I live in Washington, the "Evergreen State."

Wakefield, Michigan is a one-intersection town of twenty-five hundred people, and as blue collar as a small town can get. Everybody knows everyone else, all their family dysfunction, and every skeleton in everyone else's closet. There is no place to hide in a town like this--especially when the community pastime is to show up, unannounced, at the homes of friends and neighbors to drink coffee, or whatever, smoke cigarettes and gossip about the other fine people of Wakefield.

I experienced quite a bit of culture shock in Wakefield too. Many people in that town were just as poor as my aunt and uncle, who rented an old house that actually leaned a bit to the east. My first day at Wakefield High School was quite the event. It wasn't easy being an outsider from "the city" attempting to fit in to small town culture. The two dominant groups were the "burnouts," who all smoked Marlboro Reds and wore black leather jackets, and the popular kids, who all wore Levi's jean jackets and white Nike high-tops. It was

1985 and I was a city kid with a wardrobe purchased by my gay father. I cuffed the bottom of my jeans and wore skinny ties and boat shoes. I looked like I belonged in the cast of *The Breakfast Club*. I had the nicest clothes and best hair in Gogebic county--but I didn't fit either of the dominant groups in that school. I was a subculture of one.

What made matters worse--forgive me for saying this--the two least attractive girls in school followed me everywhere I went.

One of my family's favorite movies is *Dan In Real Life*, starring Steve Carell. Carell's character, Dan, is a widower who is set up on a blind date by his mother with Ruthie Draper. Dan is mortified that Ruthie "Pig-face" Draper, as she was known in high school, is his date, and his whole family harasses him about the set-up. They even make up an impromptu song about her. In the end, Ruthie has grown into a beautiful woman, played by Emily Blunt. It's my favorite scene in the movie.

However, in *my* "real life," "Ruthie" and her sister, "Lucy" followed me around Wakefield every day for the first several weeks I was there. Like the fictional Ruthie, I'm sure these two grew into beautiful women. But at the time it did not help my social game to have them following me around school, through town during lunch hour, and even to my home after school. I was very nice to them, but that only emboldened their pursuit. I know it is horrible to say, but nonetheless true, that they were sabotaging any social and relational hope I had of being accepted by my peers, making me socially toxic.

My Aunt Bev stood in the gap for me. She called the mother of those two girls and lovingly told her that her girls needed to back off. That was awesome. Bev knew what was up, she had my back and gave me a fighter's chance at finding some real friends.

Fortunately for me, I played sports and liked Van Halen. That, and my new Levi's jean jacket, earned me a spot with the popular jocks. Finally, after nearly two months in Wakefield, I found a place to belong.

I received an interesting call from my father that November. He had settled into a new home and found love. I will never forget how the conversation went, "Hey, Bud, I have some news for you," he said. "I want you to know that I'm gay."

What!?!?! Was he kidding me? That was made abundantly clear to me during our trip to Atlanta. I was stunned by my father's lack of awareness and his apparent need to formally announce what he had made clear to me months ago. The only words that came to mind were, "No sh--, Sherlock! I got that when trench-coat-guy flashed me at the park in Atlanta." I pulled it together to say, "Yeah, Dad. I knew that already."

He replied by saying, "You did?" with what had to be feigned surprise. Neither of us took it any further than that.

He introduced me to his new partner, Jo, and put him on the phone. I had no words for Jo other than, "What's up?" More on him later. I was so thankful to be as far away as I was. It kept me at a healthy distance from the craziness and allowed me to say, "Dad, whatever you do, don't get AIDS, okay?" He assured me he would not get AIDS. "That won't happen to me."

AIDS was relatively new on the scene in 1985 and still very much a gay man's disease. At that time, being diagnosed with AIDS was a certain death sentence. The entire nation was gripped by fear over AIDS as people were not yet sure whether it could be "caught" from someone without having sex or sharing needles. Because it was almost exclusively a gay man's disease, there were those who believed it was God's punishment on homosexuality. I confess to wondering why God left out all the gay women if he was indeed punishing homosexuality. I tried to keep it out of my mind, but I was now very worried that my dad would contract AIDS. Though he promised that he would never get AIDS, that did little to reassure me.

My best friend in Wakefield was Brian. We ran track and played baseball together. When we were not in school, we could be found in his jacked-up fire engine red 1978 Ford pickup truck cruising the backwoods and main streets of nearby towns, singing along with the Steve Miller Band, Van Halen, and the Eagles. It was a sweet ride. We loved to instigate conflicts with kids from rival schools and we could often be found at our favorite drinking spot with our girlfriends consuming the beer we had procured from Brian's twenty-four-year-old sister.

The Sting

Brian and I would often buy our lunch at the local Holiday Station (a 7-Eleven-type gas station) and drive to a spot just outside of town to eat it. When we were done eating, we would throw our soda cans and trash in the back of the truck. Sometimes we missed the truck bed--especially on windy days--leaving the trash where it landed. We were in a stretch of windy days when we pulled into our favorite lunch spot for the last time. We knew the wind had blown some of our trash on to the ground that week, but we didn't think much of it. I threw the first empty Doritos bag out the back window toward the bed of the truck. The wind caught it and it flew into the field we were parked next to. Brian threw his empty Coke can into the wind--which also missed the bed. A split-second after that can hit the ground, the door of the garage attached to the house across the street flung open to reveal a Michigan State Trooper, lights flashing, and coming at us. We were stunned to have been under surveillance. We were even more astonished to be arrested for habitually littering in that same spot. I think we may have been the only people in Wakefield to be staked out by troopers . . . that century. Our punishment was, you guessed it, a Saturday walking the highway picking up trash like a couple of proper criminals.

Because Brian and I were so close we had to have girlfriends that were close. Kim, Brian's girlfriend, was a petite girl who was spunky and tough as nails. I dated Brian's cousin, Dianne, who was tall, lanky and beautiful. She smoked cigarettes which caused her to taste of ashtray when I kissed her.

The four of us double dated to everything that year-- including the prom. Brian and I wore identical matching white tuxedos with white vests, tails, and shiny white shoes. We looked *so* good--in the most obnoxious way. We crossed

65

the state line into Wisconsin to have dinner at a supper club just outside of Hurley, Wisconsin. Though the drinking age in Wisconsin was still nineteen, it was obvious to everyone that we were four high school kids on our way to prom. But they had no issue serving us all mixed drinks and Miller Genuine Draft without ever checking our ages. We had a great time at the prom, then joined the after-party in the woods at somebody's family cabin. Dianne had to be home by 11 p.m. which meant I was riding solo at an after-party full of couples who were not looking to chat me up. My date became a case of Miller Lite which, as usual, Brian's sister had purchased for us. I don't recall how many I had, but I do recall that this was the earliest point in my life when enough was not enough for me. A definite warning sign of the addiction that was to come.

My addiction has had a sad trajectory. The first time I smoked marijuana, my dad rolled the joint for me. The first time I tried cocaine, my dad placed a small mirror full of lines in front of me. The first time I tried oxycontin, my dad offered it to ease my back pain. But the first time I got drunk I was completely alone.

I tried so desperately to play it cool when Brian and Kim dropped me off at home. I made at least five attempts at opening the front door. For the life of my drunk self, I could not understand why the door would not open all the way. It was chained. My aunt and uncle were sitting just inside watching me attempt to get through the door. I could hear my uncle chuckling, but I knew I was in serious trouble when I heard my Aunt Bev yell, *"Oh, holy hell! He's drunk!"* She was so angry and loud that I felt like the entire town learned of my intoxication in that moment.

This was the beginning of the end of my time in Wakefield. My uncle Don was "on the wagon" after years of drinking his way toward alcoholism. If there was one thing Don and Bev were not prepared to handle, it was drinking. This is the event that got my aunt and uncle talking about how difficult it really was to have an instant fifteen-year-old, with significant emotional baggage, in their home. They had my three cousins to raise--a fourth was just around the corner. That was daunting enough without all that I brought to the family. They sent me back to my dad at the end of the school year. I had been rejected and abandoned again.

Don and Bev have repeatedly asked for forgiveness for sending me back to Florida. I have never held this against them. They were doing the very best they could for their family and I'll love them forever.

MILD NEGLECT

My dad and his new, and much younger partner, Jo, had moved to Fort Lauderdale to be near the beach and the thriving South Florida gay nightclub scene. This was the beginning of a period I like to call "Mild Neglect."

I was not in Fort Lauderdale more than a few days before I realized that Jo had preferred status with my dad; something I was not prepared for. I was not coming home to my father's house as I had hoped. They had only taken me in because my parents had run out of places to send me. From this point on I would only be valuable to my dad when he and Jo were experiencing conflict. I would be his shoulder to cry on, as long as I allowed myself to be. My dad and Jo argued frequently, mostly because Jo stole money from my father to purchase drugs on a frequent basis and regularly cheated on him with the men he was getting high with. Whenever Jo misbehaved, I became my father's son again. Only then would he apologize for not being the father he should have been and look to me to prop him up and make him feel better. It often felt disingenuous and manipulative, because it was.

The first "parenting my parent" discussion with my dad came when, at sixteen years old, I told my father that as much as I would love to have a relationship with him, it would have to be a full-time mutually beneficial relationship. I would no longer be his shoulder to cry on if Jo were cheating on him or stealing from him. This was a big step for me, but my dad did not receive it well. He was both defensive and angry as he told me how ungrateful I was for all that he had done for me. All I could think was, "Is he serious? All that he's done for me has been to blow up my family, cheat on my mother, abandon my sisters and ship me to Michigan so he could have sex with whomever he wanted whenever he wanted without his son cramping his style."

****

I am the father of three daughters. I have let them down in so many ways, including falling headlong into an addiction to pain medication when they were ten, eight and three months old. Still, I cannot imagine being able to live with myself, let alone enjoy anything in life, after sending any one of them away. I can't imagine what it would take for me to be in a place where shipping my children away, in effect abandoning them, simply to give myself more freedom to live the way I want to live, would seem like my best move. I would be so overcome with guilt, shame, regret and pain that I doubt I would be able to breathe let alone feel free. I love the Elizabeth Stone quote that says, "Making the decision to have a child . . . is to decide forever to have your heart go walking around outside your body." I could no easier live without my children than I could live without my heart. I will never understand why my dad felt he would be better off without me or my sisters around him.

****

While creating boundaries for myself seemed the healthy and well-adjusted thing to do; it was purely a move of self-preservation. Feeling used by my own father, especially given our history, was more painful for me than being treated with mild neglect. From that point on, I was effectively a housemate.

I can point to my time in Fort Lauderdale as the time I began intentionally medicating my emotional pain. My dad and Jo spent most nights out on the town, which provided me a lot of freedom. I had a motorcycle and used it to stay out of the house as much as I could. When I was home, I would drink screwdrivers and smoke Marlboro Lights until I vomited. My dad didn't seem too concerned that I was drinking myself into oblivion most nights, as he was the one who suggested I switch from drinking to smoking weed because I wouldn't get sick from the marijuana.

When my dad rolled that first joint for me, I had no idea how it would affect me. I treated that joint like it was a cigarette and smoked the whole thing, at once, by myself. I'm thankful that I smoked that entire joint. It absolutely cured me of ever being a weed smoker. I experienced a very harsh high that freaked me out. I hated it. While in the throes of that harsh high, I told my dad just how terrible the experience was. I was looking for help or sympathy from him. Instead, he told Jo about it and they both had a great laugh at my expense. It was quite humiliating, but I didn't let them know that. Instead, I cursed them out then kicked them both out of my room.

"Joint" Venture

As part of fully embracing his new lifestyle, my dad had cashed out of his corporate job. He was now flush with cash that he and Jo were looking to invest in a joint business venture. Joint was most definitely the operative word--the only thing Jo brought to this venture were joints. A few weeks after I arrived in South Florida, Jo and my dad traveled the Eastern Seaboard looking for that new opportunity. They returned after ten days to announce we were moving to Washington, D.C. I was excited about the prospect of living in D.C. Even though I was still too young to vote, I had been a political junkie for years. I faked being sick when I was in fifth grade in order to watch wall to wall coverage of Ronald Reagan's inauguration--I was only ten years old. I had missed living in Chicago, so moving to a major city felt like a move that would be good for me. Plus, we would only be an hour away from the Baltimore Orioles Major League Baseball. However, it was all a lie. They told me we were moving to D.C. in the event I spoke to my mother. Because he was not paying child support, my dad wanted to keep his location a secret from my mother and her lawyer. Only after we packed up and left Fort Lauderdale did they tell me we were actually moving to Charleston, South Carolina. I felt betrayed and foolish. It was another reminder that neither I nor my feelings mattered to them at all. Charleston is the most elegant city in the United States, but I didn't know that, nor did I care. I did not want to move to Charleston.

They had purchased a One-Hour Photo shop in a small mall in the heart of Charleston's historic district. None of us suspected that choosing this particular shop at this particular time would trigger a chain of events that would impact each of us in a unique and profoundly life-altering way. It would kickstart a chain of events none of us would ever fully recover from.

When we landed in Charleston, I enrolled in Wando High School for my junior year, my third high school in as many years and as many states.

The decision to purchase the One-Hour Photo Shop was a bold choice. It would require both my dad and Jo to be on the job from 10 a.m. to 6 p.m. Monday through Saturday. I knew that would be a challenge for two self-described queens who loved the club scene. They frequently hosted after-parties at our condo until the thin hours of morning-- weeknights and weekends. My dad was willing to make partying a weekend-only thing and Jo pledged to be all in to make the shop a success, even though there was a snowball's chance he would follow through.

Jo, which is short for Jody, never had a real job. He was twenty-four and making his way through life living off an unhealthy dependence on a mother who idolized him and the benevolence of the wealthy benefactors he latched on to--primarily older men, men like my dad. It was clear that Jo was only interested in what he could gain or take from their relationship. He would never make a significant contribution to my dad, their relationship, or their business partnership. I could predict all of this from the moment I met Jody; it took my dad quite a bit longer to see it.

The One-Hour Photo Shop was in the King Street Mall on the corner of King and Calhoun streets in the heart of Charleston. It wasn't much of a mall as it only had eight shops, which included three restaurants, a video store, Kinko's, and a new age shop that kept the place smelling of earthy incense. I spent a lot of time at the mall. It didn't take long for me to find friends. As a kid from Chicago, I gravitated toward Sal, a short, fit, long-haired and loud-mouthed affable Italian-American from New York City. Sal's persona was so big that it more than made up for his diminutive stature. A long-haul trucker by trade, he moved his wife and three daughters to Charleston where he opened Custom T's, a t-shirt shop where you could have almost anything you wanted placed on a shirt.

Then there was Tony, a twenty-eight-year-old, stocky, long-haired, Rolling Stones-loving, Italian restaurateur from Philadelphia. He and his sister, Isabella, co-owned several Italian restaurants in and around Charleston, including Tramper's, the hoagie shop in the King Street Mall.

Both Sal and Tony were from big close-knit Italian families. If you were to create a stereotypical caricature of an Italian-American from the Northeast in 1986, it would look like Sal or Tony. I liked them both, instantly and immensely.

I was at the photo shop every day after school, which meant I was hanging with Tony and Sal every day. Which was more than fine with my dad as it played directly into his parenting philosophy of "mild neglect." The more I hung out with Sal and Tony, the less he had to be concerned about me.

I eventually went to work for Sal, making custom t-shirts for local sports teams, would-be gangsters, and the many tourists who visited Charleston from around the world. Our biggest customers, by far, were the College of Charleston fraternities and sororities, because our shop was in such close proximity to fraternity row. They were constantly throwing parties or hosting some event where custom t-shirts were required.

Sal and Tony were my salvation in many ways. They would also nearly be the literal death of me before my time in Charleston came to an end.

Our friendship bonded, quite innocently, at the Friday night poker games Sal hosted in the basement of his James Island home. Sal, Tony, a guy named David, and I played poker from 9 p.m. until 3 or 4 in the morning. We would then cruise over to the James Island Waffle House and have a huge breakfast together--which the winner paid for. I loved hanging with these guys and spent as much time as I could with them. Mostly because it kept me out of my own house and away from all the chaos.

Most nights, my dad and Jo would arrive home from work around 6:30 or 7 p.m. By 8:30, they were each leaning into a bathroom mirror, getting their faces as close as possible, to get their many layers and elements of make-up configured as perfectly as possible. If only I had been a daughter, I would have learned so many beauty tips from my father. I have a wife and three daughters. I can tell you that Kara and our girls do not, collectively, take as long to get their makeup on as my dad and Jo did preparing for a night on the town.

I developed quite the sense of humor to cope with the craziness of my life. I managed life with my dad and Jo, with all their drama and idiosyncrasies, by entertainingly recounting my experiences for Sal, Tony, and David at our weekly poker games. I would describe each step in a very deliberate process my dad and Jo went through when preparing for a night out--right down to how they critiqued each other's make up and wardrobe choices. I embellished a bit, but usually the straight story was all that was required. The guys nearly fell off their chairs in laughter as they listened to me tell them what my dad was like when my parents were married--dull and frumpy, just the way we liked him; and what he was like now--dyed blonde hair, skin-tight Calvin Klein jeans, flamboyant sweaters, and all that makeup. I did appreciate the fact that I wore the same size clothes as my dad and Jo. I never had to go anywhere looking shabby. Tony, Sal, and David were all good Catholics, they had never been given this level of insight into the life of gay men in America.

My three daughters never had a chance to meet their grandfather, which I grieve regularly, mostly because they have missed out on knowing one of their grandparents. Also, because knowing my dad would have helped them know my story so much better. I've had to settle for telling them as much as I can about their grandfather, and the type of relationship I had with him. When I tell them the stories, Gracie and Sophie, both teenagers, typically respond with a sarcastic, "Dad, you're such a homophobe." Not at all. I was just a teenager doing his best to cope and survive in a chaotic environment. Living with my dad and Jo gave me a tremendous tutorial about the LGBTQ+ culture, and as a pastor and a human, has caused me to care deeply about the LGBTQ+ community.

When I tell my girls the stories of living with my dad, I tell them what life was like in 1986. There was no LGBTQ+ community as we now know it. Political correctness wouldn't really take hold in the U.S. until the 1990s. Magic Johnson would not announce he was HIV positive, making AIDS a human disease rather than just a gay man's disease, for another five years. Middle and high school students were not experimenting with being gay or bisexual as being gay or "bi" was certainly not viewed as mainstream or cool the way it is in my daughters' schools in today's culture. The average American in 1986 didn't have to consider homosexuality if they didn't want to. It was still widely viewed as a life to be lived in secret and shadow. The entire country was terrified of AIDS, and gay men and women were still widely thought of as deviants. As late as the 1970s the DSM-II (Diagnostic and Statistical Manual for Mental Disorder) classified homosexuality as a diagnosable mental disorder. That stance was revised in the DSM-III that was published in 1980. It would take the nation's collective psyche decades to make that shift.

CAUGHT OR PASSED DOWN

While having a gay father brought the benefits of borrowing his top shelf clothing, it also had its drawbacks. There were several occasions where I found myself navigating the unwanted sexual advances of my dad's friends.

Buddy was a big-time disc jockey in Minneapolis who came to Charleston with his partner, Duane, to start a new Top 40 radio station. Buddy would be the station's program director and number one DJ. I thought it was cool that I knew a DJ on "The Bee," Charleston's hottest new radio station. I would often call when Buddy was on-air to make song requests while hanging out with Sal, Tony, and David. It never occurred to me that Buddy viewed my request for songs as a veiled attempt to hook up with him. The last time I called the station to ask Buddy to play a few songs, he told me that he looked forward to my calls, wished he could see more of me and asked when the two of us might get some time alone together, which he said he "craved."

As a straight sixteen-year-old kid, Buddy's request caught me completely off-guard. It never occurred to me that Buddy would make advances toward me or interpret the calls as my way of pursuing him romantically.

Had I been sending signals I was unaware of and did not intend to send? Did Buddy think I was gay simply because I lived with my dad and Jo? I confess they had a keen eye for style, so I raided their wardrobes, wore their clothes and used their cologne, but I was not sending "signals" to Buddy or anyone else. I just wanted to hear some good music. If Buddy thought I was gay simply because my dad was gay, he would not be the last person to ever wonder that about me.

When I was twenty-eight years old, Kara and I were in Miami where I was interviewing for a youth pastor position at a large church. That church treated us to a first-class experience by putting us up in a suite at the historic and prestigious Biltmore Hotel in Coral Gables. We were very excited about the potential of joining this dynamic team and we thoroughly enjoyed the diverse intercultural vibe of Miami. During one of our interview sessions, roughly halfway through the process, Kara and I were meeting with the executive team for a relaxed and casual interview. I could sense one or two of them getting uneasy as I unpacked what having and living with a gay father was like for me, and how that experience had "given me love and compassion for" gay and lesbian people. Somebody asked if I had ever "struggled" or "wrestled" with being gay myself as a result of my father being gay, or from spending as much time with him as I had. I'm sure my facial expression revealed how his question landed on me. Was this person really wondering, if not implying, that homosexuality was either passed down genetically, like red hair, or caught like a cold? It seemed both were plausible to the guy asking the question. I could feel Kara let out a deep sigh of discomfort and dismay, as I told them that it never occurred to me that I might be gay. The meeting ended with awkward smiles and a newly discovered mutual apprehension.

After the session, we broke for lunch, which gave Kara and me a chance to tour South Beach and process whether that last question represented an individual or the culture of the church. As we processed, my phone rang. It was my good friend and one of my references for this job, Dean. He told me that he had just received a call from a couple of people from the church who were asking if he ever had reason to suspect I might be gay; or have concerns about any interactions I had with kids in my care. Dean's advice to me was to enjoy the rest of our time in South Florida and run like the wind away from this job. "This is not a question you want lingering in their minds if you go to work there," he said. Which was excellent advice. I passed on that job.

ABANDONED IN THE SNOW

Nearly a year after I first met Sal and Tony, the Tucci family (Tony's family) decided to sell Tramper's and focus on their larger full-service restaurants. Tony had several interested parties, but he ended up selling his business to a couple from Colorado. When I first met William and Janet, I was struck by how obvious it was that they had never been in the hoagie business, or any business that required hands-on hard work, before. These were beautiful people with highlighted hair, spectacular tans and adorned with so much gold and diamond jewelry that it was almost offensive--and that was just William. It was curious from the very beginning as to why they purchased Tramper's. There was nothing about it that seemed to fit.

I give William and Janet all the credit they deserve for attempting to make the hoagie shop profitable. They gave it all they had to give . . . for three solid months. At the four-month mark, their tans had faded, their bling had lost its glitter, and they were exhausted. They gave up. William shut Tramper's down and presented Sal, Tony, and my father with a new business proposition, one that could make them all much wealthier.

Unbeknownst to any of us, William had been a lucrative cocaine dealer in Colorado. He and Janet had come to Charleston carrying only the "go bags" they had hidden in the event they were ever compromised and about to be arrested. They left houses, cars, furniture, and clothing behind, coming to Charleston with only a few bags filled with cash, jewelry, guns, and a few changes of clothing.

William, which I am certain was not his real name, had received a tip that he was under heavy surveillance and about to get pinched. Sensing the heat, they left everything and everyone and took off for a new life on the East Coast, where they just happened to land in the King Street Mall, and in close proximity to my life.

Janet's ex-husband was a mob insider serving a stretch in a Connecticut prison for money laundering or some such thing that I never wanted to know about. Janet's ex may have been in prison, but he could still work his connections in South Florida to provide William with some of what may have been Pablo Escobar's finest product.

William and Janet had agreed that this operation could not be run the way they had done things in Colorado. In Charleston, they would set up a system that allowed them to be at least one step removed from both the transaction and the drugs. The reason, of course, was to keep them unknown to buyers which provided an extra buffer of safety. The bigger reason for distancing themselves, however, was that William had a heavy addiction to cocaine. Janet told me stories of how William would freebase (smoke) cocaine for days at a time without sleep--Richard Pryor style. At the very zenith of a co-dependent decision, William and Janet decided that if they were going to do this in Charleston, William's hands had to be off the merchandise. Enter Tony, Sal, my dad, Jo, and ultimately, me.

The proposition was that customers would purchase cocaine directly from my dad and Jo, Sal, or Tony. No one else would know William had anything to do with this burgeoning enterprise. William would provide pre-packaged cocaine in half-gram and gram increments which would be sold for $50 and $100, respectively. Tony and Sal were immediately all in. To them this sounded like a very Italian thing to do, and they loved that Janet's ex-husband was a fellow *paisano* from New York. Unfortunately, William did not vet my dad and Jo very well at all. "Fronting" them large amounts of cocaine was the very essence of allowing the inmates to run the stinking asylum. It is impossible to give narcotics to addicts with the expectation that they will not use it, even if they stand to make tens of thousands of dollars by selling it. Not only is it impossible, but it is also slightly insane, especially if you stand to lose tens of thousands of dollars.

As if my home wasn't crazy enough, add a free-flowing supply of cocaine to the party and you had chaos every night. I was just trying to navigate high school at a time when I had zero accountability. I barely made it to my classes, and I was totally ill-equipped to deal with all the dysfunction my father brought or allowed into my life.

One of my very vivid memories from that time is of sitting at our dining room table watching dozens of people I had never seen before coming in and out of our house to sample the cocaine. It seemed everyone was getting a taste of the product but not much money was coming in. I sat at the dining room table, right in the middle of the action, because hearing it all from my room, without being able to see what was happening, terrified me.

Len Bias, who had been a star basketball player at the University of Maryland and the second overall pick by the Boston Celtics in the NBA draft that year, had died from a cocaine overdose just two days after the draft and four months prior to me sitting at that dining room table. Bias had been just twenty-two years old. He would never play a single game in the NBA.

The Len Bias Laws were passed the following year, triggering an automatic life sentence for anyone distributing drugs that were involved in the death of another person. Uh, what? Everyone around me was distributing drugs that could very easily result in their death or the death of another person. Nancy Reagan's "Just Say No" drug campaign was sweeping the nation at that time. Ironically, as a junior in high school, I had access to enough drugs to get a crash of rhinos high.

Sitting at that dining room table did not help me feel less frightened. I was terrified, because the amount of cocaine my dad consumed could easily cause him to overdose the way Len Bias had. I was terrified, with all the strange people coming and going, that gunplay was bound to break out. I was terrified the police were going to kick down the front door at any moment. I was terrified at what my life had become and where it seemed to be headed.

Fear is quite possibly the most insidious of all our emotions. It locks you down and robs you of living the life you were meant to live because your mind is constantly spinning the worst-case scenario--*for everything*. It may sound crazy, but I sat at that table because it gave me a sense of control amid the chaos of my life. I couldn't *do* anything about what was happening, but I could at least see it. That gave me a sense of control. That's how messed up things were for me.

The last time I sat at that dining room table attempting to somehow contain the uncontainable, my dad came and sat directly across from me. He dumped a pile of cocaine on a small round mirror, used a razor blade to create several lines, then snorted half of them through a rolled up twenty-dollar bill. Because I loved my dad, I want to believe he was higher than a kite when he gently slid the mirror in front of me and said, "Hey Bud, you should really try this. You're so stressed out. This will make you feel better." I was so stressed out because he was a freaking cocaine dealer! I was stressed because of the risks he was taking and the jeopardy he was putting me in!

Nancy Reagan would have been exceedingly proud of me for saying no to drugs--which is what I did three or four times as my dad insisted I "do a line."

Sadly, the last time my dad slid that mirror my way, I caved. I cut one of the remaining lines of cocaine in half and snorted it. I don't remember if I felt high or not; but I do remember the profound sadness I felt for having given in to my father. I'm feeling that sadness again as I write these words. What had I become? My father, who had helped point me to Jesus, instilled within me a passion for baseball, played pepper with me in the backyard, and at times made me feel loved and secure as a young child, was now offering to get me high.

The next morning, I woke to an empty house. There was a note on the kitchen counter from my dad which read, "Hey Bud, we had to leave. We can't tell you where we are going. Will try to be in touch soon. Love, Dad."

I was so relieved.

My dad and Jo were swimming in drug debt because they had used, and freely shared, far more cocaine than they had sold. They were tens of thousands of dollars in debt to William and flat broke. William was not a guy you wanted to be into for that much money. So they fled, leaving furniture, various possessions, the One-Hour Photo Shop, and me, behind.

I will never forget a story William once told me about a former business partner who had stolen from him. According to William that business partner ended up being murdered in a hotel room somewhere on the fringes of Baton Rouge. From the moment William told me that story until this very moment, I have believed William pulled the trigger. Which is exactly what William wanted me to think. I believe William killed that guy, with such great confidence, because of how close I would get to him after my dad and Jo skipped town.

Years later, I learned my dad and Jo had fled to a small Georgia town to stay with Jo's mother. When the money and drugs were gone, there was nothing keeping them together. Jo went in search of his next benefactor and my dad got a job as a night manager at a Valdosta area hotel.

I was now a senior in high school, without much income, who was about to be evicted. I had nowhere to go and returning to my mother in Florida wasn't something I considered for even a moment. I was certain she did not want me. I was wrong about that, but never bothered to check. The first thing I did was drop out of high school. The rent on our townhome was over ninety days late, which meant I had to get out immediately. Custom T's had a storage room where we kept supplies, a green vinyl chair and a television. That room became my home, and that chair became my bed. I was homeless.

After a few weeks, Sal and Tony convinced one of our favorite Tramper's customers to let me crash with him until we could find something better. My new roommate was John, a former enlisted Navy guy, who landed in Charleston because it was the last place he was stationed. John was a good guy, but he had sustained head trauma at some point in his life which made him erratic, unpredictable, and difficult to communicate with. He was living on disability payments and was unable to work. John was also a raging alcoholic who drank every day to soothe the many demons he believed were chasing him down. John and I lived in what had once been a beautiful nineteenth century Charleston estate. Sometime in the mid-1900s it had been turned into a quadplex of apartments, a botched surgery on an elegant home. There were two apartments upstairs and two downstairs. Each floor shared a common bathroom with three doors that did not lock. As a result, I took the fastest showers of my life and whistled while using the toilet for fear I would be walked in on by one of our neighbors. John's apartment had only one bedroom, which meant I slept on the living room floor on the world's worst futon. I was now semi-homeless.

*****

I was rescued from life on the futon by the most unlikely of saviors--William. Now that my dad and Jo were out of the picture, William wanted to restructure "the business." The first thing he did was to invite me to be a part this new venture. At first, I was certain William was drawing me close because he was hoping I might tell him where my dad had fled to. I'm still certain that was his initial motive. However, the more time William and I spent together the more he came to realize three things: We had both been royally screwed over by my father; neither of us knew where my dad was, and I was far more trustworthy, and therefore more valuable to him, than my father, Sal or Tony would ever be.

William suggested that I partner with Sal on his side of the business, but it wasn't really a suggestion. William made this move because he didn't want Sal, whose own addiction was beginning to spiral, to cost him as much money as my father had. Plus, William loved Sal and didn't want to have to kill him at some point. As a result, I was spending a lot of time with Sal and Tony once again. Which meant, among other things, that I had unlimited access to free cocaine.

Every day.

Surviving my first hit of cocaine had taken much of the healthy fear I had for the drug out of the equation. Like everyone else around me, I began using cocaine regularly to cope with the emotional pain of being alone, abandoned by my family, and terrified of being arrested, betrayed or killed at any moment.

The "reorg" of William's business meant that we would no longer be wasting energy selling small amounts of cocaine directly to the end user. It was time-consuming and dangerous, because anyone we dealt with, or any of the "friends" they were constantly introducing us to, could have been undercover police officers. We made arrangements with a few of our high-end clients to be our "distributors," who we would provide with no less than an "8-ball" (one-eighth of an ounce) at a time. They would then "step on it," or dilute it, as they saw fit, to maximize their profit. The trick, of course, was not to get greedy. If they stepped on it too much, their clients would go in search of better product. Plus, we had already stepped on the pure brick cocaine that we started with to increase our own profits.

We told our upscale clientele, with whom we had built up a solid customer base, that we were getting out of the game and referred them directly to our distributors. They never dealt directly with us again. This move meant that much of the risk and exposure inherent in supplying the user directly would be eliminated. It also meant that we would make a lot more money.

*****

One of my early mentors was Jim Burns. Jim is an author, speaker, pastor, and parental guru. I owe nearly every job I have ever been offered to the reference Jim has given on my behalf. When I was a youth pastor, I worked for Jim to train other pastors and youth workers how to address sexual identity and same-sex attraction in a biblical way.

It was 1998, and Jim, who saw that the church was not addressing this issue, was way out in front, in evangelical Christian circles, in addressing sexual identity and same-sex attraction. We were helping churches provide trained and equipped pastors and volunteers who clearly understood the dynamics, theology and science of the issue to help kids and families dealing with same-sex attraction.

*****

Several years ago, I was on vacation in Dana Point, California while Jim happened to be leading a conference for youth pastors from around the country. As I stepped quietly into the back of the ballroom to watch Jim do his thing, he saw me, stopped talking and pointed in my direction saying, "That's Todd Morrison. He used to be a *cocaine dealer*! You would never know it to look at him!" The whole room turned to look at me and then applauded. I'm not sure what they were applauding. Maybe it was that I was no longer a cocaine dealer. Maybe they were applauding sarcastically because they were all youth pastors--that's the most plausible reason. Jim didn't think I looked the part, but I had very much been a cocaine dealer and it nearly cost my freedom and life on a number of occasions.

*****

Just the other day I was sitting in the backyard with my longtime friend and mentor, Ron Rech. Ron has been like a second father to me. Though he has known me and my story for more than twenty-five years, he asked me if I had really been a drug dealer and done all the things I'm writing about in this book. I was shocked by his question; I never would have considered that someone as close to me as Ron would question my story. I asked if he thought I was lying or exaggerating. He said jokingly, "Todd, I think you may have sold a couple bags of pot when you were a kid and turned it into a great story." We laughed at his admission as I told him I wished very much that was all I had done. After a few stories from my past jogged his memory, he confessed to forgetting much of what I'd told him about myself many years ago. Like Jim Burns, Ron has known me as his kid's youth pastor who grew up to be a pastor and writer. He has even seen me in the throes of my addiction to pain medication on more than one occasion. Still, he can't imagine me as a cocaine dealer.

*****

I know I am a different kind of better because of the experiences I've had and the ways in which God has redeemed them. But, as I've told you, there is a noticeable limp to my gait; it's my brokenness, which will be with me the rest of my life. Today, I am thankful for that hitch in my step. It is an ever-present reminder of what God has rescued me from and how deep his love really is. I am thankful because I think it helps other people who are also limping their way through life to know there is hope for them too.

NARROWLY ESCAPING

It is no small miracle that I am alive to tell you this part of my story. It is a slightly lesser miracle that I was never arrested and sent to prison. There were certainly enough encounters with police where I absolutely should have been arrested, that I know God was watching out for me. Because I don't have a criminal record attached to my name, a lawyer friend of mine in Portland used to tell me not to share my stories in public as they may come back to bite me with the authorities. I can't control that, but I can say that I'm telling all there is to tell in these pages.

On one cold November night, around 2 a.m., I was walking the empty streets of downtown Charleston with roughly a quarter gram of cocaine, a snorting straw, and a few empty bags with cocaine residue in my pocket--the remnants of a typical night. Before I turned onto Meeting Street, I finished off the cocaine, and without thinking much of it, uncharacteristically dropped everything in my pockets into the drain in the gutter. The first thing I saw when I came around the corner was a police cruiser just to my left. After passing the car, I sensed it had begun to follow me. After what seemed like forever to a paranoid drug user, probably ten seconds, I heard both doors of the cruiser open and shut behind me. One second later, I heard the words, "Stop right there!"

Two of Charleston's finest, one male and one female, had some questions for me. They wanted to know what I was doing walking through the city at that hour of the morning. I told them I couldn't sleep, which was true; cocaine was, after all, a powerful stimulant. I would be awake for several more hours and would likely not sleep until sometime that afternoon. The officers did not like the answers I gave, my Chicago accent, or the fact that I did not have identification with me. So, they frisked me. Not my favorite experience. This was not at all like the apologetic TSA pat down you get at the airport. They searched everywhere for whatever they might find. What's crazy is that I was more than a little offended that they were treating me like a criminal. I certainly didn't feel like one, not yet anyway. Even though I was seventeen, I felt like a kid--a lost little boy, alone and trying to survive. I didn't feel like a criminal. Not yet anyway.

Had these two officers seen me thirty seconds earlier I would be telling a different story. I didn't recognize it at the time; but this was nearly a life-altering moment for me. Had they found cocaine residue and paraphernalia on me they would have arrested me. Who would I have called? I couldn't call Sal, Tony or William; they all had a serious allergy to the police during that season of our lives. The police would want to know where the drugs came from. At seventeen, I still had too much respect for authority and hadn't yet perfected the art of lying that would serve me so well later in my life during my untreated addiction. I get a sick feeling in my stomach when I think of what William may have done to me if I had ever been arrested and questioned by the police. I am more than confident that God wasn't saving me from the police as much as he was saving me from William.

I had a similar experience on a night I was delivering product to one of our clients in Mt. Pleasant. Getting to Mt.

Pleasant from Charleston was a quick drive over the old Cooper River Bridge, which was arch shaped with several hundred feet of clearance in the middle to allow large Navy vessels to pass beneath. Early in the new phase of the business we were wise enough to drive inconspicuous vehicles, sometimes too inconspicuous. I was driving Sal's 1976 raggedy and rusted beater of a Toyota truck. That thing had over three hundred thousand miles on it and had lost its spunk sometime around 1981. As I made my way toward the apex of the bridge, the truck sputtered, spurted and shook violently before giving up the fight and dying just a couple hundred feet from making it over the hump. I made several attempts to get across the bridge. I won't share the words I used to encourage that truck to get to the downhill side of that bridge. No such luck--it lost all momentum and stalled, every time. I was stuck. Not more than a minute later, a highway patrol car rolled up behind me with lights flashing. The trooper came to my window and asked me what the problem was. The problem was that I had an ounce of cocaine in the duffle bag on the front seat next to me and, oh by the way, I couldn't get this piece of crap truck across the stinking bridge.

"I'm not getting enough RPMs to get over the bridge," I said, with my voice, and every other part of me, shaking in terror.

******

People tell me that I seem calm and relaxed when I'm speaking publicly. I never feel that way. I'm always nervous. Once, while giving a sermon to a packed house at a Portland church, I was heckled by a guy I couldn't see. It was standing room only; I couldn't see him because he was seated on the floor in the very back of auditorium. I was mortified and completely thrown as I responded to him; but I was somehow able to speak to his issue, resolve it, and complete the sermon. Afterward, I was praised for how calmly and easily I handled such a shockingly rude interruption.

******

Apparently, I tapped into that ability to project calm while in the throes of terror on the Cooper River Bridge that night.

The officer replied, "No problem. Put it in neutral and I'll push you over the top with my push bumper."

I had no idea what a push bumper was or what it did. I could only reply with, "Okay? Thanks."

Remember, I'm still basically a kid. I was freaking out! I was certain that he was pushing me over the top so he could pull me over on the other side, write me a ticket for stalling on the bridge, discover the cocaine in the truck and take me to jail. The trooper used his push bumper to get me over the edge and followed me for two long and heart-stopping miles into Mount Pleasant. My heart was pounding through my throat as I was certain I was going to be arrested. I pulled into the first parking lot I found--certain he would follow.

To my utter shock and absolute relief, he drove right on by, missing the opportunity to make what may have been a career-advancing bust.

*****

It may seem strange to interject this here; but one of my favorite passages in the Bible is found in Psalm 37:

> *²³ The LORD directs the steps of the godly.*
> *He delights in every detail of their lives.*
> *²⁴ Though they stumble, they will never fall,*
> *for the LORD holds them by the hand.*
> *Psalm 37:23-24 (NLT)*

The godly in Psalm 37 refers to anyone who has surrendered their life to Jesus, regardless of the present condition of their life. No one who met the cocaine dealer version of me would ever have confused me for a "godly" person. Still, I absolutely believe that God protected me because he had purpose for my life beyond being a distributor of illicit drugs; a purpose that did not include an untimely death, prison time, or the burden of a felony conviction.

*****

Because our newly restructured enterprise was growing as fast as it was, we needed a central base of operations. We set up shop in the back office of Palladino's Italian Restaurant, the one the Tucci family bought when they sold Tramper's to William and Janet.

If I'm honest, I'm not sure that selling cocaine out of the back office was the craziest thing happening in that restaurant. The Tucci family had been in the restaurant business for generations in Italy, Philadelphia, and now Charleston. All those years in a high stress/high risk industry had taken its toll on some of the familial bonds. For example, Pete (or Pistol Pete as he had been known in Philadelphia in the 1950s) was the head of the family and the final authority on the restaurant. Tony's name was on everything and he ran the operation in all their restaurants, but Pete was the boss. Imagine Marlon Brando as the godfather, but with more wrinkles, less hair and the most intimidating thousand-yard stare you have ever experienced. That was Pete.

Pete and his wife Josie would often ride to the restaurant together in Pete's gold Le Baron convertible, but I do not remember ever seeing them have a conversation. Sometimes they would mumble and grunt as they were coming or going--but never with any direct eye contact. Pete sat in the first booth at the bar in the front of the restaurant, reading the paper and perpetually keeping at least three inches of ash dangling precariously from the end of his cigarette. Josie worked in the kitchen helping with prep work, cooking, washing dishes and whatever else she felt like doing. My favorite thing about having Josie in the kitchen, near our office, is that she would sing Dean Martin and Frank Sinatra songs at the top of her lungs--adding expletives as adjectives here and there. "When the moon hits your friggin' eye, like a big friggin' pizza pie, that's friggin' amore!" She was a sweetheart and I was blessed to know that she loved me. I knew it because she often referred to me as "f---ing Erick," a term of endearment meant only for family.

When we moved our cocaine operation to Palladino's, I moved in with Tony's sister, Isabella. Imagine a beautiful Italian woman with long curly hair and a smoky smooth Philadelphia accent. That was Isabella. She was not a tall woman, but she was a fierce and protective single mother raising a fantastic daughter. You didn't want to mess with Isabella. To the Tuccis I was family, an honorary Danish-Italian. So, they insisted that I take one of the rooms at Isabella's, with her daughter and their two Shar-Pei dogs. Tony was not the first, or only, drug dealer in the Tucci family. Isabella had been selling pot as a side hustle for years. Because Isabella was a bit of a hippie, she subscribed to the philosophy that if it grows in the ground or on a tree, it's natural and therefore fine to consume. She was a committed connoisseur of fine herb; cocaine was not her thing.

When our inventory ran low, William would take an Amtrak train from Charleston to Miami to meet our supplier, who I am thankful never to have met. The train was a brilliant way to transport product because there was virtually no security, multiple exits, and several stops allowing for a quick change of direction along the way. When William returned to Charleston, I would, ever so subtly, pick him up at the train station in his Porsche 928 (as in *Risky Business*) and the two of us would return to his gated community where I would get to work packaging our product.

We set up shop in William's living room. He and I sat on either side of a glass table that held the recent shipment of brick cocaine, a jug of inositol, a triple beam balance scale and William's Beretta M9 pistol. We had a rotating live shot of all the entrances to his community on the television so we would know if the police or DEA were crashing our little undertaking. We both wore surgical masks to keep us from getting utterly stoned by the dust created when breaking and mixing cocaine with inositol. Inositol was a readily available fine white powdered supplement that could be found in nearly any health store. Its color and consistency were perfect for mixing with cocaine. The packaging project required William and I to sit at that table for nearly six hours as I multiplied our product at least threefold. There is an art to "stepping on" cocaine. You must cut it enough to make the profit worth the risk you are taking; but you can't cut it so much that your customers become dissatisfied and look for another supplier. I made sure to leave a few small "rocks" of pure cocaine in each 8-ball to give our distributors the impression our product was purer than it actually was.

William came to trust me more than anyone on our four-man team or any from the group of "regulars" that often accompanied us out on the town. I never fully understood why he trusted me, given the way things had gone between him and my father. I think he knew that, out of the three options he had, I was least likely to screw him over. I think it helped him to know that I was terrified of him. Whatever it was, William trusted me and paid me a ridiculous amount of money.

Most nights we could be found at one of the popular Charleston clubs. Though I was underage, I could simply fist-bump the door man at several clubs to gain access. I never even had to bother with a fake ID. Mostly because the crew I was with made it unnecessary. We told everyone I was twenty-five, whether they believed it or not didn't really matter as my age was never an issue. The reality was, I was living on the ragged edge. I probably looked like I was forty.

Our typical night usually involved taking over part of the bar accompanied by a few people we "trusted"—usually just enough to share an 8-ball with and keep us going for a while. We drank beer with tequila chasers while passing the 8-ball between the group. When the bag was passed your way, you went into the restroom and took a hit.

If you are not afraid of drugs like cocaine you should be. I saw friends who were falling-down drunk and barely able to locate the restroom, take a hit from the bag and emerge just a few minutes later lucid and coherent as if they had not been drinking at all. It is a scary transformation.

On one of these nights, I took the bag into the men's room and inadvertently snorted what felt like half the bag all at once--which was a lot for me. One line typically did the trick. After I took that hit my nose burned, my gag reflex kicked in and I saw flashes of Len Bias in my head. One minute later, I was sweating, my heart was in my throat and beating so rapidly that I believed I was going to have a heart attack and die right there in that disgusting bathroom. I went straight to Sal and Tony to tell them what happened--they laughed. A moment later, after looking at me, they realized I might actually have a heart attack. They took me straight out through a back door so nobody would see or know what was happening. I was on the verge of losing it as I pleaded for them to take me to a hospital. They refused, telling me I would be fine once I had the chance to *walk it off*. It was in that moment, when they rolled the dice with my life to protect themselves, that I felt utterly betrayed and realized that I was completely and utterly alone in this world. These people were not really my friends; they were willing to let me die right there on the street to save themselves from having to explain what happened. When push came to shove, they didn't care about me; they cared only about themselves. They knew if they took me to the hospital, questions would be asked. Questions they did not want to answer. Questions they certainly did not want me to answer. Taking me to the hospital, in their minds, was essentially the same thing as taking me directly to the police and admitting that we were using and selling cocaine. So we walked the streets instead.

It took over an hour for me to begin to feel better. I recovered physically. Emotionally, I was devastated and acutely aware that I was on my own, abandoned again in a way which tapped into my great fear of rejection and being left out. The life of a cocaine dealer was no longer the exhilarating and adventurous life I believed it was just twenty-four hours earlier. That was the night that I realized I would most likely die or go to jail if I didn't somehow break free of this lifestyle. I knew very well that two things were true: attempting to extricate myself from all this could be very dangerous, and, even if I could get out, I had nowhere else to go.

In the years after this event, I began feeling heart palpitations. I ignored it until one night, while in my mid-twenties, the palpitations were more intense than normal and wouldn't stop. I was diagnosed with atrial fibrillation, an irregular heartbeat that can lead to stroke, heart failure and other issues. So far, I have only needed to have my heart shocked back into normal sinus rhythm twice. I can't be sure, but I point to that event in the nightclub restroom as the cause of my a-fib.

We started out keeping as much as we could about our operation under the radar. The longer we were able to avoid the authorities and the more money we made, the less concerned we became with caution. "Inconspicuous" went out the window. William drove a flashy Porsche, lived in a gated community, and kept a yacht in Charleston harbor. Tony drove around in a splashy black Corvette, which he happened to have long before any of this started; and Sal went out and purchased a vintage pearl-white Mercedes Benz E-Class.

Sal's Mercedes was a very sweet ride--when it was working. One night, while it was in the shop, he and I were making deliveries to our distributors in a Gran Torino, the sketchy loaner car from the questionable car dealership where Sal had purchased his car. As we were cruising north at fifty miles per hour on James Island's Folly Road, the front passenger-side tire came off the car! Sitting in the passenger seat, I watched as the newly liberated tire continued down Folly Road until it came to an abrupt stop by hitting a car that was turning onto the road. The tire hit the car between the front wheel and driver side door, causing significant damage to the front fender. Who thinks to check to make sure the lug nuts on a loaner are tight? I speculated that Sal's wife may have loosened them after discovering Sal's affair with one of our clients . . . I still do. No doubt she wanted Sal dead for cheating and me dead for hiding it from her.

There was no way we were going to avoid police involvement. "We are going to jail," was all I could think. Sal blurted out a few colorful words in both English and Italian, obviously concerned about that very thing. He looked at me with terror in his eyes and said, "Be cool, kid." The last thing I could have possibly been was cool. We had enough cocaine in the car to light up the entire city of Charleston for the weekend.

Sal and I made our way to retrieve our tire and talk to the driver who was now in possession of it. "Holy sh--!" were the first words out of the driver's mouth when he saw us. He said it again, asked us if we were okay, and then introduced himself by the very same name that was embroidered on his jacket--Big Lar. It turned out Big Lar was from Chicago, coincidentally, just like me. I don't know how or why what happened next came about. Maybe it was simply three Yankees from big cities meeting up in the deep south under unique circumstances that created the instant bond between us. Maybe Big Lar had some contraband in his car too? I'll never know. What I do know is that Sal and I made a new friend that night. After a few quick Chicago connections were made between Big Lar and me, Sal pulled out a wad of cash, offered $2,500 to our new friend and said,

"Big Lar, we don't need to involve insurance or police, do we?" "Hell no; we don't!" he said as he quickly stuffed the cash in his pocket.

When the police arrived, it was all I could do not to kneel down, cross my ankles and put my arms behind my head to be fitted for handcuffs. But Sal, Big Lar and I all played it far cooler than we felt. The police were put at ease by the fact that we were all getting along so well. They took our statements, asked us where we were going (we lied), wrote Sal a ticket for "failing to secure a wheel," or some such thing, and left without any idea they had just missed out on a major cocaine bust. A bust that would have pointed them to William and triggered arrests and property seizures that would have made their careers. Instead of going to jail, Sal and I reattached our wayward tire, double-checked the other three, and went about our evening business.

That night, which began with an accident which led to nearly being arrested and having my life turned upside down, ended like every night during that season of my life. We resupplied our distributors, met up with friends at a club where we offset our drinking with regular hits of cocaine, took the party to someone's house after the clubs closed, and landed in bed sometime between 5 and 7 a.m. My routine was the same each day. I would throw my head face first into my pillow wishing I were somewhere else and wondering how I could get out of the life I felt stuck in. I was so miserable that I even resorted to praying. "God, we used to know each other. If you are still here; get me out of this, please!" Only to wake up sometime that afternoon to rinse and repeat the process. Which I would do again the next day, and the next. I was making a ton of money, but I was desperate to trade it all for a less dangerous life where I could be loved for who I was rather than the party I could provide.

It was about this time, when all the days seemed to blur into each other, that I received a call from my dad. The news he shared may not have been shocking, but it was devastating. He had been diagnosed with full-blown AIDS.

It was 1987 and AIDS was a disease that had profound personal, relational, and societal implications in America. Worst of all, anyone diagnosed with AIDS in the 1980s could expect an agonizingly tortuous, social, emotional and physical descent into a horrible death.

I don't recall the details of this particular conversation with my dad, but I do recall believing this would be the last time we would speak and that I would never see my father again. The conversation between us was short and it was clear to everyone around me that the news of my dad's AIDS diagnosis had leveled me. I was angry with him because he had abandoned me, twice! But he was still my father and I had never stopped loving him.

My "friends" did what these types of friends do. William gave me a fifth of the most expensive scotch he could find while Sal and Tony gave me cocaine. None of it helped. The drugs had betrayed me as they ultimately do. They were no longer providing the required effect to dull the senses, elevate my mood, and soothe the ache in my soul.

Things around me began to unravel. William had fallen completely off the wagon. Once again, he was going on cocaine benders that would last for days. He was so shredded that it was nearly impossible to communicate with him. He got it together for a few days, however, when Janet announced she was leaving him. She simply could not watch William destroy himself again. Because we were so self-absorbed, no one in our crew noticed that Janet had descended into the throes of raging alcoholism herself. She was at, or very near, rock bottom when she reached out to trusted friends in Denver for help. They did not have to do much to convince her to return to Colorado. William resigned himself to the fact that she was leaving, but he would not allow her to drive from Charleston to Denver alone; I would be the one to drive her. This was my punishment for being the one William trusted most.

The drive to Denver was miserable for several reasons. I didn't want to babysit Janet or be the delivery boy who got her home safely. The weather was miserable as snow and sleet were falling as far south as Baton Rouge, Louisiana and Dallas, Texas--which meant that instead of taking a two-day journey on Interstate 40 through the middle of the country, we would have to take Interstate 20, the southernmost route, which added an extra day to the trip. It was slow and dangerous as snow and sleet covered most of the route--in places where they were ill-equipped to remove snow and sleet from the roadway. The whole thing was quite stressful for Janet. She started drinking the moment we left Charleston and did not stop, even after we reached Denver. William paid me well to escort Janet to Denver, but Janet was not checking in with William as he had asked her to. It didn't occur to me that I needed to check in with him. In hindsight, I should have. He was so out of his mind paranoid that he pinned me up against the wall when I returned from Denver and demanded an answer to the question, "Did you sleep with her?!"

If I had slept with Janet, William's method of extracting information from me would not have elicited an honest response. No, I had not slept with Janet! As messed up as things were in our lives, Janet became a type of motherly figure in my life. In fact, Janet was older than my mother. Sleeping with her would have been wrong and weird on so many levels.

By this time, what started off as an exciting and lucrative endeavor had become a wasteland of personal, marital, and relational wreckage for everyone involved. Sal ended up leaving his wife and three lovely daughters in his beautiful James Island home in favor of withdrawing and isolating in a run-down motel room, adjacent to a bowling alley, with Lydia, the woman he said he loved. I thought Lydia was only there as long as the drugs were there. She was beautiful, fun to be around and someone not to mess around with. I liked Lydia very much, but like the rest of the people around me, she was an untreated cocaine addict who would do whatever it took to get high. I witnessed her steal cocaine from us at a time when there was no need to do so. Sal was providing her with all the cocaine she needed. However, for an addict, enough is never enough--it takes one to know one. She stole from us in an attempt to hide how much cocaine she was really using and to make sure she wasn't solely dependent on what Sal supplied her with. Of course, when I asked her about it, she denied stealing anything and made up an elaborate story as to where the cocaine had gone. Lydia was constantly attempting to seduce me, in an attempt to get even more cocaine, even though I was Sal's closest friend, ten years younger than her, and had confronted her about the cocaine she had stolen from him. She was sucking the life out of Sal at a time when he had so little life to give.

One afternoon, after spending hours at a local bar attempting to drown the sorrow of his family breakup, Sal arrived at the t-shirt shop by nearly driving his Mercedes through the Kinko's lobby next door. He left the car where it landed, at a forty-five-degree angle to the street, about two feet from the Kinko's window with three tires on the sidewalk and one on the street. He stumbled into the t-shirt shop, mumbling and incoherently drunk. He located an 8-ball of cocaine and laid out a line that appeared to be fourteen inches long. Within a couple of minutes of snorting that line, Sal was lucid, coherent and fully functional. Though he'd spent the afternoon drinking Jack and Coke until he was falling down drunk and had just inhaled roughly half a gram of cocaine--he appeared to be stone cold sober. This remains one of the most dramatic and physically impressive transformations I have ever witnessed a human being go through. Sal was spiraling into the oblivion of a full-blown addiction to alcohol and cocaine. It was brutal to watch. I confess I did nothing but enable it.

William was medicating the pain of losing Janet with vast amounts of alcohol, cocaine, and sex with women much younger than he was. He became quite reckless as he would often bring the various women he was seeing close to the inner workings of our operation. Tony was the only one of the adults in my life who seemed to maintain some judgment and reason in the midst of the chaos. He had his family business to run, which meant he couldn't afford to let cocaine get the best of him. He was the only one who did not have an emotional relationship with cocaine. He enjoyed it as much as anyone, but he maintained a business mindset about the whole thing. Cocaine was a product Tony sold, not a friend he could not live without.

Our little operation was sliding off the rails.

ALTERED TRAJECTORY

Late in the summer of 1988, I made a phone call to my uncle in Chicago that would forever alter the direction of my life. He told me that my grandfather had cancer and was not likely to live another six weeks. I was devastated. My grandfather had been my rock and one of the great spiritual influences in my life. If not for him, I would never have been searching for God in the thin hours of the morning and crying out for him to rescue me in my despair.

My grandfather was born Sven Peter Christensen on the rural Danish island of Jutland in 1905. At the age of nineteen he boarded a ship with his childhood friend Nels, bound for New York City. Sven and Nels would pass through Ellis Island like more than 12 million other immigrants looking for a better life in America than they left behind in their home countries. Soon after arriving in America, my grandfather would do all he could to Americanize and acclimate himself to his adopted homeland. For example, he started going by his middle name, Peter, and became an American citizen as soon as he qualified to do so. Going by Sven would have left him open to greater prejudice than the name Peter. Even though he would carry a thick Danish accent the rest of his life, changing his name made a huge difference in how people treated him--simply because most people knew other guys named Peter. Not many knew anyone named Sven.

In many ways, my grandfather lived the American Dream. Among other things, he became a very successful door-to-door Fuller Brush salesman who carved out a great living for himself even though he never went to college. He was able to provide all my mother, my uncle Pete and my grandmother needed, and so much more. Upon hearing that my grandfather was dying, I immediately made plans to travel to Chicago to see him.

When I arrived at my grandfather's house, a place I had been a thousand times, a bolt of panic shot through me. "What was I doing there? What would I say to my grandpa? What would he say to me?" I couldn't possibly tell him anything about my life, could I?" It got very real for me as I prepared to knock on the door. I didn't know if my grandfather would be glad to see me or disappointed in me. His wife, Hedy, who had been my nanny in Copenhagen and married my grandfather four years after my grandmother's death, greeted me at the door and escorted me to his bedside. Outside, it was a brilliant late September day; inside, Hedy had drawn all the shades such that darkness and death seemed to linger in the air, ready and waiting to take my grandfather away.

His body had been ravaged by cancer. He was lying in his bed a shell of his former self. I had no words. I had no idea what to say. I knew this would be the last conversation he and I would ever have, but I couldn't speak. I was overcome . . . with shame . . . with sadness . . . with guilt. I was overcome by the wave of grief that hit me as I sat at the bedside of the only hero I knew in my life at that time.

We sat in silence long enough to make it awkward. Finally, my grandfather broke the silence with his tears. He stretched his hand to my knee and began weeping as he repeated the words, "I am so sorry. I am so sorry, Erick."

He was inconsolable. My grandfather needed just one look at me to recognize I was living on the ragged edge, and it broke his heart. He didn't know the half of what was actually happening in my life, but he knew enough to weep over my condition. I could never have imagined he would react this way. I wasn't prepared for such a selfless demonstration of love. He was the one suffering and dying, yet his heart broke over the pain he could see in my eyes.

Suddenly, this expression of love became very personal for me. I understood this was a holy moment.

This was the type of experience we may only be blessed with once in our lives if we are fortunate. But it took more than five years for me to begin to understand what this moment meant to *my* life. I'm still coming to grips with its significance. On his deathbed, my grandfather became a living expression of Jesus to my broken life. His pain and suffering were profound. Yet, somehow, he looked beyond his suffering and impending death to weep over the suffering he discerned in my life. He had far more insight into my pain and condition than I had in that moment. What an extraordinary gift that was! A selfless and life-altering offering to a seventeen-year-old kid who didn't deserve it, but so desperately needed it. God was answering those desperate prayers I had cried into my pillow night after night in Charleston, hoping that he was real and listening. He was real, he was there, and he had been listening. . . and he used my grandfather to rescue me.

I emerged from that encounter with my grandfather with a clarity I had not previously possessed. I was not alone. My life mattered and had purpose! I needed to get it together so I could discover what that purpose was. If I stayed in the cocaine business one of two outcomes was certain to play out: death or incarceration. Maybe both. That night I made calls to William, Tony, and Sal telling them that I wanted out and planned to move to Chicago. There were two problems with my plan; I didn't have a place to live in Chicago and leaving an operation like ours could put everyone associated with it in jeopardy.

Before I returned to Charleston to attempt to extricate myself from our crew, I visited my uncle Pete at the five-acre estate he enjoyed--by himself. I was certain my uncle would put me up long enough for me to get my life together. I told him everything. I told him about the "business" I was involved in and made sure he understood that if I stayed in Charleston, I would end up dead or in prison. I begged him through tears to let me live with him so I could escape the fate that awaited me in Charleston. Unlike his father, my Uncle Pete was unmoved by my brokenness, my pleading or my tears. "Sorry, Scooter," he said, "I can't do it. I'm a bachelor, pal. I live alone." I was devastated, as I interpreted his "no" as my own uncle, my flesh and blood, saying he would rather see me dead or in jail than be inconvenienced by my presence in his house.

Two days later, I was preparing to return to Charleston when my uncle told me he had changed his mind. He said that he had shared my situation with his oldest friend, Jerry Grumbles, who I had always known as a gruff trucker with a grumpy disposition. Grumbles helped him realize that if he couldn't help a family member in need, he wasn't worth much. Thank you, Jerry Grumbles!

Years later, at a dinner among friends near our home outside Seattle, my friend Evan Ujiye asked me if I could point to a single event or defining moment that altered the trajectory of my life. Yes! It was this encounter with my grandfather.

EXIT STRATEGY

Nobody in our Charleston crew wanted to see me leave. They initially took the fact that I had some kind of "spiritual awakening" during my trip to Chicago as a threat. They were afraid I would feel compelled to confess my sins to the authorities and put them all in jail. That was the business reaction; the personal reaction was just as strong and just the opposite. The fact that I was attempting to break free and get my life together caused everyone else to take a quick inventory of their own lives, which none of them wanted to do. Most of their lives and relationships had spiraled into disaster or crashed and burned. It was easier for them to remain in denial about all the wreckage and pain they had caused. They would have preferred that I remain in denial as well. Misery does indeed love company. Still, they knew they were ruining my life and needed to let me go.

My role in the business meant that I knew everything there was to know about our little organization. I knew of the incarcerated mobster in Connecticut who brokered our cocaine deals in South Florida. I knew our methods of transport and distribution. And, most troubling, I knew the names, addresses and phone numbers of each one of our "distributors." The only thing I did not know was where William stored our inventory after I cut, weighed, and packaged it--no one knew that. Yet, all of that was nothing compared to what I knew about William, Tony, and Sal, individually. We had enough dirt on each other that, if ever it came to it, we could all likely broker an immunity deal in exchange for sharing the information we had on each other--all the illegal extracurricular shenanigans that took place on the periphery of our cocaine operation.

William by far had the most to risk, and to lose, by letting me leave. As his trusted sidekick, I could have easily burned him to the ground. Fortunately for them, they knew I loved each one of them in my dysfunctional little family. I had no intention or desire to burn anyone to the ground. I just wanted to go home to Chicago and begin living my life.

I was glad to be getting out when I did. However, had I faced prosecution, I doubt very much the authorities would have treated me as a minor. I was just seventeen years old, the youngest of any of us, or of any the people we associated with, by several years. They all knew they had been contributing to the profound delinquency of a minor for the better part of two years. William, Tony, and Sal were each playing a knowing and active role in ruining both my present and my future. Fortunately for me, each one of those guys, as well as those in our inner circle, actually cared about me. I was "the kid," as they called me, and for whatever reason, I had gained their trust and admiration. They would have let me die on the street rather than take me to the hospital, but they loved me in their own highly dysfunctional way.

The most unexpected goodbye came from Pistol Pete Tucci. He hadn't said more than five sentences to me in the time I knew him; I was terrified of him. Yet, the day before I left, Pete came over to me, looked me dead in the face with that thousand-yard stare of his, and said, "Erick, you are family. Don't ever forget that. Family! Wherever you go and whatever you do, this is your family!"

I wasn't sure whether to hug him or thank him. I didn't want to ruin the moment, so I replied, "Thanks, Pete. That means so much. It feels like family." I always wondered how much he knew about the business we had been running out of the back office of his restaurant. I think he knew way more than he let on.

Josie's goodbye was a little different. "Well, kid . . . " she said with her arms open and a tear in her eye. "Get the f--- out of here already, would ya? Come on, you're killin' me over here. Go!" She hugged me, tightly and longer than expected, then turned and wept with her entire body as she left the restaurant. This was Josie's way of telling me how much she loved and would miss me. It was as touching as it was eloquent. She was one of a kind.

So much of my time with these people had felt like family. A highly dysfunctional alcoholic, abusive, and criminally oriented family. But family, nonetheless.

They were all sad to see me go, even Pete and Josie. Yet each person on our crew would experience a vicarious freedom in my departure. They couldn't get out, but they could celebrate *my* newfound freedom. They blessed my departure by throwing a huge party on William's yacht in Charleston harbor. I left for Chicago the next day.

Panic Sets In

During my last days in Charleston, I reached out to my mother, who I had not spoken to in more than two years. I reached out to her because I felt like I was breaking free of a life I was ashamed of in favor of something new and good. When she learned I was moving to Chicago, she brought my two younger sisters to Charleston to see me. I was so happy to see my family, especially my sisters. I was completely unprepared, however, to have my cocaine world collide with my family world. When they came to dinner at Palladino's I went into a full-blown panic attack. It felt as if my soul had fractured. I could not find my breath or my bearings. Everything was out of sync and I absolutely lost it as I curled up in the corner of the office bathroom hiding from everyone and everything. This panic attack was total confirmation that I was unhealthy. I had buried my pain, anger, shame, sense of loss and betrayal, and so much more, deep in the inner recesses of my soul. As happy as I was to see my mother and sisters, I didn't have a clue how to be with them in that environment. So, I hid from them. Which I regret to this very day, mostly because of the message it sent to my sisters. I am sure I made them feel unimportant, unloved and discarded. I hadn't been there for them when they needed me. I had been in Michigan while they endured my parent's divorce, and all that went with it, without their big brother there to protect them. Now, when I had the chance to attempt to make it right, I didn't know what to say or what to do. I failed them. I was a criminal and a huge disappointment. Thankfully, there would be other occasions and opportunities for us to reconcile--but not in Charleston, not under those circumstances.

Home at Last

I landed in Chicago on Saturday, October 1, two days before my eighteenth birthday. I kept in touch with the crew in Charleston. It was clear that they missed me. William even tried to get me to return, offering me more money and promising to introduce me to some cute girls he'd just met. Not a chance. I was *home*, exactly where I was supposed to be. I chatted with William, Sal and Tony quite a bit during the first few weeks I was in Chicago. Then, quite suddenly, everything went silent on their end. After another couple of weeks went by, Tony called me. "We got busted!" he said with bewilderment still in his voice. He seemed disoriented and anxious as he recounted the story of how the police raided their homes and businesses just three weeks after I left Charleston. He and William had been arrested in a sting operation that had been in the works for months.

William had, quite brilliantly, stashed all his cocaine in a car he kept in a random "guest" stall inside his gated community. He purchased the car with cash, so it would be extremely difficult to trace back to him. Wisely, he would only go to the car alone in the early morning hours to ensure he would not be seen. Unfortunately, William was not as brilliant or discerning about some of the women he allowed to get close to him. After Janet left him, William pursued women with great fervor, as though he were on some type of conquest. There were several women in and out of his house. So many that I gave up on learning their names and who they were because I knew they would not be around long. They were all very nice, very beautiful and very young--at least twenty years younger than William, who must have been in his late forties, even though he said he was thirty-seven. He could be quite charming, but most of these women weren't exactly smitten with William. They were there for the fun, the money, the yacht, and the free cocaine.

It was the last woman William brought near that delivered the death blow to our organization. Whether she was an informant before she started dating William or became one after realizing what she had stepped into, we will never know. But we do know that William got sloppy. Unbeknownst to him, this woman followed him to the car and watched as he retrieved a significant amount of cocaine from inside the back seat. She then shared this information with the authorities, giving them the last, but crucial, bit of information they needed to make their case against William and Tony. Sal had submerged into oblivion, in that motel room with Lydia, and fallen off the radar of any of the authorities.

My friends and former colleagues never had a chance. They were caught completely off-guard and served up on a silver platter as the government seized property, cash, weapons, and cocaine. In Tony's case, they seized property, including his Corvette, that he owned long before going into business with William.

Amazingly, William, who was the big fish in all of this, was granted bail, which he happily, and quite easily, posted just before he skipped town, never to be seen again. I am at a complete loss as to how or why William was granted bail. Maybe he had a great lawyer or an incompetent judge--maybe both. Maybe he paid somebody to arrange bail. That would not surprise me in the least. I wonder if the most likely scenario is that William went into the witness protection program. William had to keep himself out of prison to preserve his life. Unlike the rest of us, William had direct interactions with the mob and, very likely, representatives of Pablo Escobar's enterprise. In other words, people who may have killed him if he were in a position to share how, where and from whom he got the cocaine we sold in and around Charleston. As inherently dangerous as our work was, William never seemed concerned that he would be arrested. He was prepared for it; just as he had been in Colorado. In the end, just as he and Janet had done in Colorado, William somehow grabbed his "go bag" and none of us saw or heard from him again, which has been just fine with me.

Tony arranged for plea deals which assured he would not serve any real jail time. I lost touch with Sal in 1989. I reached out to Tony in 2007; he had married one of the ladies who had frequented our inner circle and they were about to celebrate their twentieth year together. He was still running a Charleston area restaurant where you can probably still get the best Italian food in town.

I recently connected with Sal after searching social media for those I'm writing about but have lost touch with. I was so glad to hear from him--mostly because I was sure he was most likely dead. It has been fun to reconnect and share stories of where we've both been these last three decades. I have to admit I was absolutely shocked when Sal told me he reconnected with Lydia six years ago--twenty-six years after their cocaine-fueled affair. Sal tells me they are both clean and sober and loving life together. I'm thrilled for them both!

I often think how different my life would have turned out if I had remained in Charleston just a few weeks longer. I would have faced a felony drug charge, likely as an adult. I would have carried that the rest of my life; into every relationship I ever pursued and every job application I ever filled out. I am quite certain I would not be married to Kara, the father of my precious girls, or the pastor of anything. I sometimes ask the "what if" questions of my life: What if I had not been compelled to visit my grandfather in Chicago? What if he had never wept over my brokenness? What if Uncle Pete hadn't changed his mind about taking me in? I feel my heart rate increase and the knot in my stomach tighten as I consider the various paths my life could have taken. I am so grateful to have exited the cocaine operation when I did, and I am very grateful for what I have in my life today.

I can tell you, without any doubt, that God rescued me in my brokenness and spared me from creating and experiencing even greater wreckage in my life. That is what God does . . . he is in the business of going to great lengths to rescue broken and brokenhearted people from despair-- even the despair of their own doing.

COMING HOME AGAIN

Back in Chicago, I connected with several of my childhood friends; but many of them, including Becky and Joy, were away at college. Most of my local friends were heavily involved at Moraine Valley Church, where my family attended just prior to moving to Florida. My friend Shaun was on my case more than any of them about coming back to church--something I was completely unprepared for and unwilling to do. I gave Shaun any number of excuses for why church would not work for me. The truth was, I had great memories of Moraine Valley Church and the people there. I was longing for the type of connection and relationship I once had at that church--but that was a long time ago. A lot had happened in my life since I was last at church. I was terrified of returning to Moraine Valley because I believed that the moment I walked into that church the religious people would take one look at me, smell the cigarette smoke on my clothes and judge me as both worthless and unlovable--all without saying a word. I was convinced that is what religious people were like. My fear of rejection was on high alert around church people, so I stayed away from Moraine Valley as long as I could.

Somewhat hypocritically, I used the network of relationships I still maintained with people from that church to search for a job. I landed a temp job working at Waste Management in Chicago Ridge. The job was to spend October and November walking the streets of Naperville alongside a streetsweeper while using the vacuum boom from atop the truck to suck up the leaves residents had raked into one large continuous pile at the curb. The job required me to wake up at 5 a.m. and get home at 6 p.m. Having a real job and working for a living was quite the shock to my system. But I loved it. I did such a good job sucking leaves in Naperville that Waste Management hired me to work full-time. I was still three years too young to drive a garbage or recycling truck, but they put me to work anyway in and around the yard. It was the dream job for an eighteen-year-old kid as most days I could be found at the wheel of a forklift, tractor, roll-off truck or earthmover. I landed that job through Craig Phillips, one of the Sunday School teachers and AWANA leaders I had known as a kid. Craig was a rising star on the Waste Management executive team, destined to run his own shop. Even Craig got on my case about going to church, as did the other guys he'd hired from Moraine Valley Church. It was a divine conspiracy that I could not get away from.

It was just before Christmas 1988, when Shaun invited me to join his family at one of the Christmas Eve services at church. Shaun said, "Hey, Erick. Come to church with us, man! Even people like *you* go to church on Christmas!"

He convinced me that I could show up and fly under the radar like all the other people who only showed up at church on Christmas or Easter. I was terrified, even as I was about to walk into a church I'd been to hundreds of times as a kid. I remember taking a deep breath just before attempting to sneak in one of the side doors. I had not been in the building for more than thirty seconds when I heard someone say, "Erick!" It was the Dave and Lenore Denison--parents of an old friend I hadn't seen in years. I was blown away that they remembered me. They asked me where I had been, what I had been up to and how my family was doing. I lied. In church.

The Denisons were not the only people to remember me or to hug me that night. I certainly was not prepared for the emotional experience I had my first time back at that church. It was as if I had come home to Moraine Valley Church and everyone was genuinely glad to see me.

As it turned out, Moraine Valley was going through what I call an "awakening of grace." They were making it their mission to tap into the inexhaustible grace of Jesus, drink deeply of it, and lavish it on to the lives of those they encountered. The wonder I experienced upon stepping back into that church was as unexpected as it was amazing. It was powerful and compelling, and it drew me in. They didn't judge me based on what I looked like, what I had done, or for smoking the cigarettes they could smell on me. They simply lived out their authentic relationships with Jesus and each other and allowed me to belong until I was ready to believe.

One Sunday, after a church service ended, Don and Bonnie McLaren, Shaun's parents who had known me since I was eight or nine, asked if they could pray for me. I didn't know why they wanted to pray for me and honestly, I was not at all comfortable with the idea--but they weren't really asking. They were going to pray for me whether I was comfortable with it or not! I don't remember what they said to God on my behalf, but I will always remember the absolute joy, peace and love I felt afterward. As I walked the hundred or so yards from the building to my car, I might as well have been walking on air--in fact, that is exactly what it felt like. I was not looking for it or expecting it, but I was overcome by what I now know to be the relentlessly tender love of Jesus that had been pursuing me my whole life--as a child in Copenhagen terrified that my parents were fighting; while driving through Atlanta with my father; while being abandoned and shipped off to relatives; even as I lived wildly selling cocaine in Charleston. Jesus had been pursuing me.

Two families in particular, the Langans and the McLarens, unbeknownst to one another, told me that I was now part of their family. When it was a holiday or a birthday, or whatever--I was invited. Their love for me slowly melted my defenses until I was ready to share my story with them. When I told them where I had been and what I had done, in all of its awful, ugly and illegal detail. they simply said, "We figured it was something like that. We love you no matter what you've done and no matter where you have been."

I believed them. The way those families, and that church, loved me back into a relationship with Jesus was nothing short of amazing. It was powerful and transformative. The experience of being welcomed, loved and allowed to belong, as I was and not as I, or anyone in that church, thought I should be, was a great gift. That unconditional love and acceptance blew me away and was, without a doubt, the biggest influence on my decision to step back into a relationship with Jesus. How those families, and that church, treated me has been the single biggest influence on, and shaper of, my philosophy of ministry. I am passionate about leading the church to proactively love broken people who are desperate for healing, hope mercy, grace, and forgiveness by allowing them to belong until they are ready to believe.

The love that church showed me was so powerful that I surrendered my life to Jesus--whatever he wanted me to do, I would do. I pursued the next indicated step in my spiritual journey, baptism. I was slightly terrified to take this step because it meant that I would have to give my testimony in front of the entire Moraine Valley Church. These days I'm known for being transparent and vulnerable about my present, my past, my failings and my addiction. But that is now. Back then, the fear of being judged was very real. It was one thing to share my story with the families who loved me. I trusted them and was secure in my relationship with all of them. It was something altogether more complex to share it with fifteen hundred people--while standing in a small pool of warm water. It took some time, but I found my courage and committed to getting baptized.

The baptism was set to take place during one of the Wednesday night prayer services, which meant there would only be four hundred people present. There were people there that night who had known my parents, heard bits of my story and had come to show their support for me. Their presence meant a great deal to me, but I was still terrified about sharing my story. Thankfully, Pastor Bill Johnson was in the baptismal tank with me. He was Marian Johnson's husband, and like his wife, he was a huge advocate and great ally in my life. I was so nervous about what I would say that I stepped into the tank of water and immediately, almost instinctively, grabbed the wired microphone to begin sharing my testimony. All four hundred people gasped in horror as they expected to see Pastor Bill and I electrocuted right before their eyes. Talk about a surge of the spirit! That would have been a prayer meeting for the ages! One thoughtful gentleman from the front row ran up and grabbed the microphone out of my left hand before I had the chance to transfer it to my wet right hand, thereby putting an abrupt end to the night and what would have been the most memorable baptism in the history of Moraine Valley Church. I confess, that near-death episode took away most of the fear I had about telling them what a disaster my life had been and how lost I felt before stepping through the doors of that church the Christmas before. I was able to tell them how thankful I was to have walked into a love I had never known but had been searching for my entire life.

Not only had they loved me back into a relationship with Jesus, they also helped me discover my purpose and my passion. Rick Wager, the youth pastor at Moraine Valley, saw leadership qualities in me that I would have never seen in, or believed about, myself. He and others in the church offered me real leadership opportunities and prepared me to be a leader. When Rick first talked to me about volunteering in the high school ministry, I said, "Sure, but I will only do games. You don't want me doing anything spiritual with people, I'll just screw them up." So, I did games for a few months.

In late 1989, just a year removed from partying on William's yacht in Charleston Harbor, Rick approached me about being one of three adult leaders on a high school mission trip to Haiti. After that trip, he arranged for me to be the staff director at the summer camp that several Chicago area churches attended in Northern Wisconsin. My role was to oversee roughly one-hundred high school and college age students who spent the summer working jobs such as lifeguard, counselor, wrangler, and kitchen duty at the camp. I was just nineteen and in way over my head, but it was a great experience. Even better, I was the ski boat driver. Everyday Kurt Wilson, the lead lifeguard and I, would grab a few people and tear it up on Lake Sawyer while the campers were doing crafts and eating lunch. I became a novice leader and an expert slalom water skier that summer. Rick and his brother Dave Wager, along with the other leaders they connected me with helped me identify what I was good at, what I loved to do and the calling on my life. For that I am forever grateful to those two guys!

GUILT AND CONSEQUENCE

Because of the things I have done, the places I have been, and the impact my worst actions have had on the ones I dearly love--guilt and shame often accompany me as I make my way through life and recovery. They come uninvited and unexpectedly to torture me for hurting not only myself, but others--even those I do not know and will never know. Recently, I watched a documentary on Pablo Escobar with my teenage daughter, Gracie. Escobar was a horrific human being who reigned over Bogota, Columbia with a murderous terror that made Al Capone look like a Sunday School teacher. I was not prepared for the wave of post-traumatic stress that hit me as I watched Pablo's biography. I can't be certain, of course, but in the late 1980s, William was getting our cocaine from South Florida at the same time the Escobar cartel smuggled more cocaine into Miami than any other cartel by far.

Before seeing the documentary, I told my cocaine dealing stories to friends and churches as evidence of God's intervening mercy in my life--and for their entertainment value. After watching the documentary, I had to ask myself whether I had become indifferent to the damage I had done and the wreckage I contributed to, not only in my life but in the lives of so many others--including the people of Bogota who suffered immensely under Escobar's influence. Watching Escobar's story triggered a wave of fresh sadness, regret and culpability to wash over me because I had indirectly and unknowingly supported a lunatic murderous drug lord.

Three years after leaving Charleston, I was a student at the University of Northwestern in the Twin Cities of Minneapolis and Saint Paul. I had a breakfast meeting with a youth pastor who was interviewing me for a volunteer leadership position in the youth ministry he led at a large Minneapolis church. After hearing my Charleston drug dealing stories, he told me that I would likely age faster and die younger than those who had not sinned to the degree I had sinned. Not only did I feel an unhealthy sense of shame, I regretted telling this guy my story. I was now wondering if God would really treat me the way this youth pastor told me he would. Was I only partially forgiven by God for my sin? It felt like this guy was saying God pulled a "Gotcha!" on me. Yes, Todd, you are forgiven, *but* your punishment is premature balding, wrinkles and an early grave. Really? Would God now be holding a grudge against me for the rest of what I had just learned would be my much shorter life? I took what this youth pastor told me to heart because he was forty and I was twenty. He was the expert on God and religion; I was just a college student with a messed-up history. His words spun me out for a while until I realized that the only problem with his theology was that it was wrong. Unfortunately, it took me years to come to this realization.

His thinking was what I'll call "hierarchy of sin" theology which states that certain sin, typically that which is public, obvious and unable to hide or be kept hidden, has a greater consequence and/or punishment than other, not so obvious sin. Hierarchy of sin theology tends to completely leave out the insidiously evil nature of sins that are done in secret and kept hidden, sometimes for generations.

Hierarchy of sin theology sees abortion, homosexuality, addiction, and divorce, for example, as unforgivable, conditionally forgivable, and/or less forgivable sins than others. I have sinned far greater, and with much deeper consequence to myself and others, in my active addiction to pain meds than I ever did when I was a teenage cocaine dealer--and I did some terrible things in Charleston. Not only that, if my record could be expunged of my cocaine years in Charleston and my years battling addiction to pain meds, I would still be one of the most horrific sinners in the history of the world. My secret sins of lust, lying, cheating, judgment, character assassination, manipulation, etc., etc., etc. have done profound damage to myself and others. The die was cast on my soul without adding criminal or addict to my list of offenses. While certain behavior has greater real time and real-world consequence than other behavior, there is no hierarchy of sin. In Romans 6, the Apostle Paul tells us that the penalty for sin is death. Not just the worst of sins, but all sin. The spiritual consequence of all sin is separation from God--death. Whether we tell a white lie or commit murder the spiritual consequence is separation from God, which is death. The wonderfully great news is that Jesus forgives our sin, all of it, and brings us back into an unbreakable relationship with God--forever.

ANGELS AND A LOVE BOOT

Even after I got out of Charleston, got a job in Chicago, and went about my life, I had no intention of ever reuniting with my father. Still, I felt the weight of his absence, and often wondered where he might be and how he was doing. In the quiet moments, I found myself wondering whether he was dead or alive. If he was alive, I wondered, how badly was he suffering from the effects of AIDS? It took four years and the significant influence of my girlfriend, Kara, for me to seriously consider the whereabouts of my father, and to care enough about that relationship and the condition of my own soul to go in search of him.

I started dating Kara when we were both students at the University of Northwestern. To put it bluntly, I was oblivious that Kara was pursuing me. It didn't help that her initial pick-up line was to ask me if I wanted to help fix her broken down Toyota truck.

"No, sorry. I have an unfortunate history with Toyota trucks," was my response. I wasn't even swayed by the bumper sticker on her truck that read, *My Boss Is a Jewish Carpenter.*

A couple of weeks later, Kara and I would attend the same concert on the Northwestern campus--each with someone else as our date. It worked out kind of like that scene in *When Harry Met Sally*, when Harry and Sally (played by Billy Crystal and Meg Ryan) set each other up with their best friends on a double date. The match was a total misfire and Harry's date leaves with Sally's date. Somehow, over the course of the night, my date started talking with Kara's date and I started talking with Kara, in the end, everyone left happier than when they arrived.

Being somewhat of a Casanova, I put together a noodles and sauce gourmet dinner, complete with garlic toast, made by two girls who lived in my dorm, for our first date. After dinner we went to the Minneapolis Sculpture Gardens--outdoors in Minnesota, in the middle of February. It was roughly eight degrees and Kara and I were both struggling not to slip and fall as we traversed the icy garden terrain. I reached out my arm in a gentlemanly gesture to help Kara through an icy patch--she promptly rejected my help, evidence that my work was most definitely cut out for me. She was not just going to fall into my arms and head over heels in love with me. Our first date was an epic disaster but fortunately, not a deal breaker, as she agreed to a second date, stipulating it must take place indoors. Over the next several weeks, we hung out around campus and went on many dates. Although Kara possessed quite the independent streak, I thought things were going very well between us and that a promising relationship was taking flight.

In mid-March, less than a month into the relationship, Kara suddenly, and without notice, broke up with me. I was shocked and deeply wounded as this came straight out of the blue with no warning signs. To add insult to serious injury, she cited "no sparks" as the reason. *Ouch!* For the next two weeks, I was a heart-broken mope walking around campus looking as though someone had stolen my puppy. What was most troubling about our breakup was my conviction that there had been lots of sparks between us--Bobby Brady kisses Millicent and gets the mumps, Fourth of July, God

Bless America-type fireworks! How could she say there were "no sparks?" There were most definitely sparks, and she knew it.

As it turned out, we had a mutual friend, Steve, who, like me, was a huge baseball fan. He bought tickets for six or eight of us to attend opening night of the 1991 Minnesota Twins baseball season. The Metrodome in downtown Minneapolis was packed with nearly sixty-thousand fans cheering on a Twins team that would go on to win the World Series that year. In a stroke of divine intervention, Kara's seat number was right next to mine. We sat in the left field bleachers as we watched one of the best baseball games I have ever been to, on what would turn out to be one of the most memorable nights of my life.

The Twins were playing the California Angels whose star player, Dave Winfield, a Minneapolis native, had a game for the ages. Winfield had the only three home run game of his Hall of Fame career that night. Eleven years later, I ran into Winfield at the Manhattan Club in New York City. I so desperately wanted to go up to him and tell him I had been at the game in Minnesota when he hit three homers. But I chickened out. He was a Hall-of-Famer, with his family, and probably on vacation. A knucklehead like me saying, "Hey, I was one of sixty-thousand people at that game" seemed . . . well, stupid. Which is why I'm writing about it. Mr. Winfield, if you happen to be reading this, I WAS AT THAT GAME! I would love to talk to you about it sometime.

As awesome as Dave Winfield's three home runs were, it was Kirby Puckett's only home run of the night that changed the trajectory of two young lives in the left field seats. Everybody knew it was gone off the crack of the bat. As it carried toward the left field seats, the ball seemed like it was coming right at me. I caught it on a fly--but not the way you may be thinking. The ball initially sailed just over my head, went through the hands of a fan sitting two rows behind me, bounced off his face, breaking his glasses and possibly his nose, and right into my hands.

It was awesome!

I stood on my chair holding the ball in the air for a ridiculous and inappropriate length of time. I was soaking in every bit of Jumbotron airtime I could get. Just before I sat down, I noticed I was standing on a piece of glass. It was a lens from the glasses of the poor guy two rows behind me. I picked it up, turned around and asked if anyone had lost a lens. "Yeah," said the guy, as he attempted to rest his broken glasses on his bloodied nose. Puckett's home run had hit him right between the eyes.

"Can I at least have the ball?" he asked, in the defeated voice of a man coming to grips with his colossal whiff. You can't blame the guy for hoping to come away from such an embarrassing event with something to show for it, right?

"Nope! Sorry, man . . . can't do it" was my response. This baseball would serve a greater purpose than to ease that guy's pain.

Sitting right behind me were a little boy and his dad. The boy, who looked to be about nine years old, brought his baseball glove to the game for one purpose--to catch a home run off the bat of Kirby Puckett, the Twins superstar centerfielder. He was pounding the pocket of that glove with the frustration of being one seat away from fulfilling his lifelong dream. The two of them reminded me of the many times I sat in the outfield seats at Comiskey Park in Chicago with my dad, my glove in hand hoping to catch a home run off the bat of Carlton Fisk or Harold Baines. It only took one look at the kid sitting behind me to decide what to do. I whispered "watch this" to Kara as I turned around and handed Kirby's home run ball to that little kid. His face lit up with exuberance as he examined every stitch and scuff of his most valuable possession. I'll never forget the kid's father leaning forward to say, "Thank you so much. Can I buy you and your girlfriend a beer or something?"

I didn't care about the beer; he called Kara my *girlfriend*! She could have corrected him by saying, "We're just friends." But she didn't. In my mind she was leaving the door open to the possibility that there were, in fact, sparks between us.

Kara and I spent the rest of the game talking, laughing, and thoroughly enjoying each other's company. So much so that we ended up at the Eagle's Nest, a burger place on campus, until the early hours of the morning. The later it got the more serious our conversation became. We were comparing our hopes and dreams for the future and describing the type of person we would each like to end up with. Our intended futures were lining up quite nicely. So nicely, in fact, that at what I thought was just the right moment, I leaned over and kissed Kara.

It was a really sweet kiss. Not too long and not too much. Mouth closed. When the kiss was over, however, there was a look on Kara's face that I did not quite recognize.

She got up from the table, walked over to the nearest trash receptacle and *vomited*!

I had never had that effect on a woman before. I was slightly stunned as I watched this unfold. I did not get up to hold her hair back, nor did I offer her a napkin to wipe her mouth when it was over. I just sat there thinking, "Huh! *I guess there were sparks after all!*" I knew right then that this was the woman I wanted to spend the rest of my life with.

Kara hates it when I tell this story. I have her permission but not her blessing to share it with you. People always want to know why she vomited. Was she sick? Had she had a bad hot dog at the game? No. She was nervous. She had broken up with me because she did not want to be in a serious relationship. She threw up after I kissed her because she was coming to grips with the reality that this was a serious relationship, and she was into it.

I would also have to come to grips with how serious this relationship was, and what that would require of me. There was a specific day, about three months into our relationship, that I came to the realization that I had fallen in love with Kara. It was that same day I felt the greatest conviction I may have ever felt about anything--I would have done anything to get out from under the weight of it--because of what it demanded of me. Kara and I were spending a weekend with her parents at the lakeside home that belonged to longtime friends of Kara's family. I knew I had to tell Kara the story of my life. I had to tell her about my family, my dad, the drug years in Charleston, the women I had known-- all of it. I won't lie to you, I considered all of my options, including not telling her. I knew that someone with my history and baggage was not on her, or her parents', approved list to marry. I looked for any way to make it easier, softer, and somehow less terrifying--for her and for me. Could I leave some of it out? No. I could not leave any of it out and ever ask or expect her to trust me. I had to tell her, and I had to tell her everything. I was terrified.

It terrified me to tell her because I knew it was not the story she was expecting from the man she would fall in love with. It was not a story she expected to hear from a fellow student at a conservative Christian college where Billy Graham had once been President. Nobody at a school like the University of Northwestern had stories like mine--not that they shared, anyway. It terrified me because I knew that I came with a lot of baggage and I could not fault Kara if she didn't want to take it all on.

I remember sitting down with her on the shore of one of Minnesota's ten-thousand lakes and laying out all the sordid details of my life up to that point. She cried, of course. She cried for quite a while before taking some time to think about whether she would fully give herself to this relationship. Part of her processing was to talk with her parents--which was painfully difficult for me as they certainly didn't need more information or, as I saw it, ammunition, to steer their only daughter away from this city kid they weren't totally convinced was good enough before they heard my story. To their credit they left the decision to Kara. When she came back to me with her decision, I was nervous and probably visibly shaking. I loved this girl and didn't want to lose her. I was shocked at her words, "God told me to love you." Well, you can't argue with that!

That was Spring and Summer of 1991. I am writing these words just over twenty-nine years later. Since that memorable first kiss, we have enjoyed wondrous seasons of blessing and peace; and we have endured hellacious events that tested the faith and resolve of us both. We have experienced the highs of marital bliss and the lows of wanting out of the marriage. We fought through it, both literally and figuratively, to get to where we are today. We are still far from perfect. If we held a marriage conference it would be all about what not to do. Still, in our nearly thirty years together, we are fiercely committed to one another and to bettering ourselves, our marriage and our family. And, thankfully, we have arrived at a place where Kara only occasionally vomits when I kiss her.

Kara is a country girl who grew up on a dairy farm in Wisconsin. Dairy farming is a tough business. Cows must be milked twice per day, every day--no exceptions. Dairy farming never allows for a day off. As a result, Kara is tough. She has needed that toughness to stay with me and put up with my shenanigans these many years. I learned early on in our marriage that when Kara sets her mind to do something, no matter how challenging it may be, she follows through. It was that tough dairy farmer determination, combined with her tender and compassionate heart, that partnered with me in search of my father.

Kara was able to sense the gaping void in my life where my father should have been. I knew it was there, but I was doing my best to bury it and defer, or deny, whatever impact it was having on my life.

New Beginning

Before Kara would officially agree to marry me, she wanted to meet my family. She wanted to have her own firsthand, up close, and personal experience with my family of origin--which included my father. Kara wanted to take this trip as much for herself as for me, which I felt was more than fair.

I had not seen my father in four years, and it had been nearly three since I last saw my mother or my sisters. This would be a brutal trip for me as I would be unable to be with my family and keep my feelings about my history with them buried in the inaccessible recesses of my soul.

Only six years earlier, my parents had agreed to ship me off to relatives in Michigan. As far as I was concerned, they gave up on me when they made that decision . . . they abandoned me. As a result, something within me broke that had yet begun to heal. The capstone to a highly unstable childhood, which embedded within me a profound fear of abandonment, was that my parents made my greatest fear a reality. One of my glaring character defects and sources of great pain in my life has been FOBLO (Fear of Being Left Out). FOBLO has worked in concert with my many other flaws to create a healthy amount of wreckage in my past-- mostly in the years between my teens and late twenties when I had no idea that my fear was running unchecked across the landscape of my life. FOBLO is still with me and it still rears its ugly head from time to time. Taking a trip to see my family and to find the father who had abandoned me *twice*, was an anxiety-riddled journey back to my childhood I was not eager to take.

As expected, the trip to Tallahassee was painful, but it laid the foundation for future, much improved, relationships with my entire family. I loved introducing Kara to my sisters. Like me, they have been the recipients of collateral damage from my parents' divorce, and they suffered greatly from the way our father abandoned them too. My mother was very angry with me for having lived with my father in Charleston. She saw the time I spent with my dad as a declaration of my unequivocal love, devotion, and support for my father. It hurt her deeply that I had never offered any of that to her. Of course, that makes sense to me now, but it never occurred to me then. I hadn't really offered my dad any of those things. I was just a kid trying to survive. My mother's anger toward me did not stop her from loving Kara, of course. She loved Kara instantly and immensely. Fortunately for me, she couldn't love and be in relationship with Kara and remain as angry with me as she had been. It would take several years, the death of my father, and the arrival of her second husband, David, for my mother to forgive me for having a relationship with my dad after their divorce.

Sadly, my mother and I are still not that close-- relationally or geographically. We see each other only every few years and connect by phone on holidays and birthdays. She and David remain in Tallahassee. We live in Seattle. There is still quite a distance between us.

It was on that pre-marital family reunion trip to Florida that my sister, Hannah, got word that my dad was in a rehabilitation facility near Valdosta, Georgia. To this day,

I'm not exactly sure what type of rehab facility it was. I believed it was a mental health facility as, ironically, my twenty-year-old self had no idea of the need for various types of rehabilitation facilities--including those for alcohol and drug addiction.

The fact that he had AIDS had me preparing for the worst. I was surprised he had lived as long as he had, and I expected him to look as though he were near death. When my father emerged from his "wing," I barely recognized him. He was as thin as I had ever seen him. As he moved toward us, his gait seemed to be fatigued and defeated. Of course, he was as sharply dressed as ever. No matter how terrible my dad may have felt, and no matter where he was, he would always put himself together. In this case, however, he couldn't hide the fact that his body was breaking down or that it was taking its toll on every part of him. He looked sad, which moved me to feel quite sorry for him.

I treated that meeting as though it would be the last time I would see or speak to my father. I did my best to try to let go of any anger and pain I was feeling over his leaving me to fend for myself back in Charleston. That was difficult to do because I had not yet allowed myself to feel or address any of that pain he had caused in my life. He was tearful, sincerely apologetic, and intensely thankful that I had come from Minnesota to see him. He was especially thankful to meet Kara and to learn that marriage was in our future.

My dad would beat the odds and the data by living another ten years before succumbing to the ravaging effects of Acquired Immune Deficiency Syndrome. This reconnection with my dad served as the foundation of a rebirth of our relationship. Like everyone else in my family, my dad loved Kara immediately and immensely. For Kara, the feeling was more than mutual. The relationship the two of them would forge over the next ten years would go a long way in helping me address and work through the deepest points of pain in my relationship with my father. A relationship that would never be as close as it had once been, but would eventually be as healthy as it could possibly be. In the years that followed, my father went above and beyond in asking for forgiveness and trying to reconcile and restore our relationship. We had many tearful conversations in which I felt like I was parenting my parent--again. He hoped for a clean slate. I had to tell him that a clean slate could never be possible as a lot of damage had been done in a past that could not be relived or revised. We could only do the best we could given all that had transpired between us. We would have to rebuild trust, reestablish boundaries, seek and extend forgiveness, address and acknowledge points of pain, and see where we landed--all with the clock ticking on his life.

LIVING WITH AIDS

My father lived with full-blown AIDS for no less than fourteen years. This was quite an amazing feat, given the reality that several of his friends, whom I had known, had been diagnosed around the same time as my dad and died within two years of their diagnoses. Some of that had to do with how advanced the disease was when those men received an official diagnosis. Much of it had to do with the reality that AIDS was a death sentence, a punishing social stigma, and a painfully horrific way to die. Several of my dad's friends medicated their emotional and physical pain with massive amounts of drugs and alcohol. The effects of the disease itself, combined with that of the drugs and alcohol, hastened their tragic and premature deaths.

My dad wanted to live. He would later tell me that he wanted to extend his life enough to give him the chance to reunite with all three of his children--something he never quite achieved. My youngest sister, Rachel, never really knew her father. He traveled quite a bit when she was younger, and she was just five years old when my parents divorced. It wasn't fair to Rachel, or realistic, for my dad to push a relationship on her as there had never been much of a connection between them. Rachel had always been closest to my mother, which was very good for both of them. She and my mom were able to build a strong bond, an alliance, in which each promised to look out for the other.

Treatment for AIDS was in its infancy when my dad received his diagnosis. He did not trust that his doctors knew enough about the disease or how to treat it to follow their advice. He may have been right. So, he dedicated himself to studying the disease--new treatments and emerging therapies, and most importantly, the side effects of the medication he was prescribed. At the time, the side effects of the medication for AIDS could easily kill you before the disease itself had a chance to run its course. It was his commitment, even when the internet was in its infancy, to educate himself and self-medicate that helped prolong his life. Amazingly, however, my dad would periodically undermine his efforts to remain alive by relapsing with various uses of cocaine, including smoking it. As much as he wanted to live, knowing that he was going to die at a relatively young age was sometimes too much for him to bear.

Kara and I did all we could to make the most of the time we had with my dad. We understood that every trip we took from Chicago, and later from Seattle, to see him could very well be our last. So, we made it a priority to visit my dad, and the rest of my family in Tallahassee, every Spring, Summer and Thanksgiving.

Groupthink

In those early years, Kara and I were living in Chicago while I was attending seminary at Trinity International University and working as a vastly underpaid part-time youth pastor. I followed in my parents' footsteps by going to a Christian College and earning a Bible degree. Unlike my parents, I had no intention of going into ministry, so I also earned a degree in Psychology from the University of Northwestern.

In fact, there was a time when I thought I would be an accountant. Those of you who know me are laughing right now, and rightfully so. I hated accounting and I was terrible at it. The best "accounting" I did was to take the $57.00 accounting book back to the campus bookstore for a full refund after dropping the class. After getting my money back, I walked through the commons area of Prairie State College, a community college in Chicago Heights, Illinois, and for whatever reason, I spoke these words out loud, "Okay, God. I'm not going to be an accountant, but I'm not going into ministry." As usual, God got the last laugh.

In the early years of our new relationship, my dad absolutely loved the fact that I was going to seminary and working in a church. It wasn't so much that he was proud of me as it was his opportunity to test me, challenge my faith, and question the religious institutions I was affiliated with. Every time we visited my dad, he presented us with a new "challenge."

On one visit early in our marriage, my dad asked if we could take a family portrait that would include my sister Hannah and her infant daughter, Alyssa. My dad made it abundantly clear that we would be using a photographer friend of his who was great at what she did and happened to be a lesbian.

My dad would later ask me how I felt, as a Christian and a pastor, about paying a lesbian to take our family portrait. Honestly, at the time I was conflicted about it. Even though I had lived with my dad and been surrounded by gay men and women, some of whom had become my friends; my internal pendulum had swung to the point of aligning with the viewpoint toward homosexuality that many Christians held. I was judgmental and believed that interacting with them, by paying a gay woman to take our picture, was somehow a violation of my religion. As such, I responded to my father's questions the way I believed my religious affiliations expected me to respond. Sadly, I put more effort into aligning with those affiliations than into how I should respond as a follower of Jesus. I told my dad that being a lesbian was sinful and that I wished he had not felt the need to go out of his way to put me in such an awkward position. I knew better. I knew that being a woman who is attracted to other women is not in and of itself sinful. But I didn't consider that, nor was I willing to. I was making the same broad-brushed judgment other Christians often mistakenly make, which serves to alienate same-sex attracted people from the church, and, more importantly, from Jesus. I wish I knew then what I know now. I wish I had been more like Jesus.

One of the traditions Kara and I developed with my father was to spend every Thanksgiving with him in Tallahassee. Until the end of his life, my dad was constantly working out his theology and attempting to land in a spot where he felt he and God could get along. The longer he lived, the more humble, contrite and penitent he became. He spent a few years attending the Metropolitan Community Church, which was founded in 1968 as a church for LGBTQ+ who didn't believe they had a place in other churches. During one of our visits to Florida, my dad invited Kara and me to attend a Thanksgiving dinner at his church on the Wednesday before Thanksgiving. It was quite the experience for an evangelical pastor, as it looked, felt, and sounded just like my church. The "churchy" language was the same and the prayers, prayed to God the Father in the name of Jesus, sounded as sincere and heartfelt as those prayed in my church. The only difference I could be sure of was that nearly everyone at Metropolitan Community Church was gay.

We had dinner at a table with my dad and two other gay couples. One couple were women who had adopted two young boys. The boys, who both looked to be about six years old, were also seated at our table. While it is fairly common to see same-sex couples with children in today's America, it was very uncommon in 1993.

My dad had not orchestrated the seating chart for the dinner, but he could not have been more thrilled about the serendipitous nature of things. He effectively interviewed the parents of the two little boys seated with us; asking them how they came to adopt, whether they were both called "mom," and what challenges they faced as a same-sex couple at places likes soccer games and PTA meetings. After dinner, we had not been in the car two minutes before my dad was grilling me about how I felt about having dinner with a lesbian family. He really wanted to know what I thought about the fact that a gay couple had chosen to be parents. I remember having mixed emotions, but I was definitely not in favor of it. My concern was that the two boys we had met that night would have an unbalanced childhood. They would grow up without a father in their life, and their worldview would be profoundly skewed by seeing homosexuality as "normal." Ultimately, I feared these things would preclude them from ever discovering a relationship with Jesus. Even if they decided to go to church, how likely would it be that they would attend a church that openly shares the gospel of Jesus and the story of God as found in the Bible? I didn't think it was very likely as very few gay people, gay couples, or gay families attend evangelical churches that openly share the gospel of Jesus and the story of God as told in the Bible.

I remember my dad asking me a question that did not change my mind that night but has profoundly influenced my thinking since. My dad asked me if I thought it was better for those two boys to bounce around in the foster care system alone or have a home where they were both loved and provided for by a couple that happened to be gay. My answer revealed my conviction and my ignorance. I told my dad that neither situation was great for those two boys. Which was a total cop-out of a non-answer. I was quick to judge as a young seminarian. In doing so, to my shame, I withheld the love of Jesus from those who needed it every bit as much as I did. I was not willing or able to live in the tension of loving and caring for those who do not believe what I do, but matter every bit as much to Jesus.

THE GOOD DOCTOR

In early 1993, my dad met Doctor Earnest Edwards of Tifton, Georgia, a man my dad would later refer to as the love of his life. Earnest held a doctoral degree in music from Florida State University and after many years of teaching, was employed as the part-time pianist and organist at a large Baptist Church in southern Georgia. I have always believed that this church probably had a "don't ask, don't tell" policy, as the U.S. armed forces once did. Either that or it was the most progressive Southern Baptist church in America, and the first to employ an openly gay man in such a public role. The Edwards family had been a prominent family in that Georgia town, and they had been members at that church for generations. As such, it was most likely that the church did not have any real choice about Earnest's role without significant consequence from his stakeholder family.

I first met Earnest when he accompanied my dad on a trip to visit Kara and me in Chicago. We would meet the new couple at Cite, a very chic restaurant atop Lakepoint Tower on the shores of Lake Michigan in downtown Chicago. Though my dad had given me a heads-up, I was caught a bit off guard by the age difference between him and Earnest. My dad was forty-four, Earnest was sixty-six. From the very beginning, their relationship had the hint of a "father and son meets gay couple" vibe to it. The dynamics may have been unusual, and there may have been many years between them, but it was clear that these two men loved each other very much, and though it wasn't legal for them to marry, they would end up caring for one another until death did, ultimately, separate them.

I am forever grateful to Earnest for being in my dad's life. Unlike Jo, and some of the other men in my father's life, Earnest loved my dad, which was very reassuring to a son who lived three thousand miles away. Earnest provided an exceptionally loving and high level of care for my dad as his health declined. I saw the pain and tears in Earnest's eyes during the many conversations we had about how best to deal with my dad's declining health. I saw it when we made plans for the funeral, and I saw it in the way he mourned my father's death. Being with my dad in sickness and in health was exactly what Earnest wanted to do. Sadly, there was never much health during their years together.

We loved Earnest, though he was far from perfect. He was a borderline alcoholic who loved his gin and tonic. In fact, gin and tonic became my drink of choice because of the time we spent with Earnest. In his advancing years, Earnest experienced a lot of physical pain, for which he was prescribed oxycodone and other pain killers. Earnest would often mix his oxycodone with his gin and tonic, which sometimes caused him to do things he would have never done otherwise. One such occasion was Thanksgiving 1997.

Chocolate Foot Cream

We had enjoyed another great Thanksgiving dinner with my family at a restaurant called Julie's Place, our Tallahassee Thanksgiving tradition. We had all eaten so much turkey and stuffing that we decided to take our dessert home to enjoy later--cheesecake with sides of chocolate sauce. My dad and Earnest retired to their bedroom for the night around 8:45 p.m. while Kara and I sat on the living room couch enjoying a movie. Around 9:30 p.m. we heard Earnest moving about the kitchen, apparently looking for something in the refrigerator. A few minutes later, he emerged from the kitchen wearing nothing but a robe that he had not bothered to cinch up. By this point, he had consumed several oxycodone tablets and gin and tonics and was not in complete control of his faculties. As he sat on the coffee table directly across from me, I made sure not to break eye contact for fear of what I might see. He completely disregarded Kara's presence in the room as he held out a side of chocolate sauce from Julie's Place in his right hand. With the slurred speech of an elegant Southern gentlemen, he spoke these words to me, "My dear, I brought this foot cream for you. I thought you might enjoy it if I massage your feet."

I was as ill-prepared to respond as I was shocked by all that was unfolding before me. The only thing I could think to say was, "Earnest, that's not foot cream, it's chocolate sauce--and I am pretty sure *you're drunk!*"

Earnest had an extraordinarily confused look on his face as he considered both what I had said and what he was holding in his hand. We could see the flash of clarity pierce his foggy mind as his eyes widened to the reality of the situation. He shot up from the coffee table and darted quickly back into the safety of the bedroom. Kara and I had no words. We could only look at one another in utter bewilderment.

Two minutes later, my dad emerged from the bedroom with a curious smirk on his face. "What the hell just happened out here?" he asked smiling with great anticipation.

I told him, "Earnest wanted to massage my feet with *chocolate sauce*. That's what the hell just happened out here!"

My dad loved it! For his money, this was way better than hiring the lesbian photographer or meeting the lesbian moms! He was thoroughly entertained that his straight pastor son had been put in such an awkward position. The fact that Earnest had done it was icing on his cake--maybe chocolate sauce on his cheesecake.

My dad apologized to Kara, of course. She will never be able to unsee any of what she witnessed that evening. However, it was of no concern to my father that I, too, would never be able to unsee Earnest, in all his glory, sitting on that table offering to lather my feet in chocolate. He was too busy reveling in my misfortune to care.

All I could say to Kara was, "Welcome to my family, Babe."

Earnest left for Georgia early the next morning. We did not see him again on that trip. I would be lying if I said I wasn't smiling right now as I tell you this story. There was so much wrong, unhealthy and sad about that encounter with Earnest. He was overmedicated and abusing both alcohol and his pain medication. The truth is that though Earnest was "blacked out" and would never fully recall the events of that night, he made amends to Kara and me. It was far from a traumatic event, but it was part of what being in relationship with my dad brought to our lives. Though it was embarrassing to Earnest, Kara, and me in the moment, we got past it and we moved on. We loved Earnest before this encounter, and we loved him just as much when it was over.

Good Versus Great

Some of our friends don't know what to do with this story. They are also the ones who struggle when they hear me say that I am "thankful" for Earnest.

I loved my father, and I am so thankful for the relationship I had with him those last ten years of his life. So much healing took place, especially in those final years, as my father recognized the pain and deep wounds his choices caused and the lasting impact they had on his children. I don't know if my father ever reached out to my mother; he spoke of wanting to ask for her forgiveness too. I don't know if my mother would have received that very well; my guess is that it would have, initially, caused her more pain--but it would have been the right thing for my dad to do. As far as my thoughts on my dad's relationship with Earnest: Though I loved Earnest, I never believed that my dad's relationship with Earnest was the *best* outcome for anyone. The best outcome for my family would have been for my parents to have had a strong marriage; for my dad never to have been gay, and for my sisters and I never to have experienced such profound brokenness as children--brokenness that still lingers deep within us. There were a few bells of pain and tragedy in all our lives that could never be unrung. The trauma occurred, and the damage was done no matter how remorseful my father may have been. Still, because my dad and I were both committed to reconciliation, we had to do the best we could to piece the wreckage back together. Our lives and relationships would never regain their original shine, that was certain. Still, real reconciliation did take place between my dad and me. I was very thankful to have Earnest in my dad's life--and in my life for that matter. Kara and I both grew to trust Earnest and to love him deeply--chocolate sauce notwithstanding.

As a pastor, I have had many parents and family members who have heard my story, seek counsel on how to navigate a relationship with their gay child, sibling or loved one. I have journeyed with parents who were absolutely divided on whether they should cut relational ties with their gay son or daughter. These were good people . . . *Christians* . . . stuck in the agonizing tension between loving their children and not wanting to condone, or appear to be condoning, sin. Loving someone and remaining in relationship with them does not have to mean that we condone everything about their behavior, their choices, or their lifestyle. Our sons, our daughters, and our loved ones can discern this. They will never be confused about our convictions, even if we choose to be in their life. In my experience, they would prefer a relationship with us, knowing we don't condone their choices, over being alienated or abandoned by us.

When It's Someone *You* Love

Kara and I had known our friends, John and Claire, for nearly twenty years before a major change occurred in our relationship. John and Claire moved to Seattle from England when John was hired at Microsoft. We became fast friends who enjoyed hanging out, going to concerts, and taking in the occasional Mariners game together. There's nothing like the looks you get from other baseball fans when they hear a British accent sharing insights on the finer points of the game--or explaining the rules of baseball to other Brits. During my time as a pastor at Westminster Chapel in Bellevue, Washington, John and Claire partnered with me by stepping into key leadership roles as we launched a dynamic ministry to young adults. When they moved back to England several years ago, it left a huge void in our lives. Fortunately, John was able to stay with Microsoft in the U.K., which provided a way for us to see him several times each year.

In the summer of 2018, John and I were scheduled to have dinner together during one of his trips to Microsoft headquarters in Redmond. The morning of our appointment, John texted me to inform me that he would be sending an email he wanted me to read before we met that night. I was a bit freaked out, as John and I never had any trouble saying hard things to each other. I knew he had been quite ill in recent months and that the team of doctors who had been running him through a gauntlet of tests, were considering things like lupus and cancer. I was certain John's email was going to inform me that he was gravely ill. That was the only thing I could think of that John would struggle to tell me in person. I was wrong.

John's email informed me that he had been dealing with gender dysphoria his entire life. For as long as he could remember, he felt that his proper, or true, gender was female. As a result, the email went on to tell me, I would be meeting with John for the last time that night. If, after learning this, I still wished to remain in the relationship, it would no longer be with John. Going forward, my friendship would be with Hope.

I was so relieved it wasn't cancer! I also felt a bit of sadness that he had kept this from me for so long--though I certainly understood why he had.

When I shared this much of the story with a pastor friend of mine, he asked, "Did you stand true to your convictions or did you choose to be in relationship with your friend?" My answer was, "yes" to both. Kara and I could never stop loving our friend, especially when there was so much that we did not know or understand about her choice.

Kara and I have stayed in relationship with Hope and Claire, who are still happily married. None of this was a surprise to Claire. In fact, when John became Hope, Claire was relieved because she no longer had to hide the fact that she loved Hope every bit as much as she had loved John. John shared his gender dysphoria with Claire prior to their engagement, over twenty-five years ago. Claire chose to stay in the relationship with the love of her life many years ago. Some of the people who have heard this story wonder if we have theological differences with Hope and Claire. Yes. Do we believe that we share a common and life-changing faith in Jesus with them? They confess to believing so, yes. I admit that I don't exactly know how to reconcile it all or what the future holds. But I do know that Hope and Claire desire to follow Jesus and have desired to help others know and follow Jesus as well.

There have been some who wonder why we would stay in relationship with Hope and Claire. The answer is easy, we love them dearly. What would we accomplish, other than hurting our dear friends, by breaking off the relationship? It is impossible to be an expression of the love and hope of Jesus to people we have cut out of our lives. Hope and Claire are true friends who have been there for Kara and me through thick and thin. They have seen me at my worst, in the throes of addiction and the depths of clinical depression. Yet, while they may have been justified in doing so, they did not cut me loose. They loved me then and they love me now. What kind of hypocrite would I be to break off our relationship? Especially when the people who are wounding Hope and Claire and their two children the most right now are religious people--many of whom don't know them, their faith journey or their story. I stand with my friends--to love them, to attempt to understand what I don't yet understand, and hopefully to be half the expression of Jesus in their lives that they have been to me. I believe that is what Jesus would do and I believe it is what he would have me do.

For nine months from Fall 2000 to Spring 2001, Kara and I were in Indiana helping a church in the Indianapolis suburbs work through a season of transition. It was there that I met Mark, a sophomore in high school, who was a follower of Jesus, gay and suicidal. Mark heard me share my story at church one Sunday and took the risk to believe I might be safe enough to reach out to. The first time Mark and I met, he told me that he desperately wanted to follow Jesus, but felt he was failing because he could not stop himself from being gay. In the wake of some unfortunate, albeit well intentioned, and damaging counsel, Mark believed he would have to stop being gay and feeling gay in order to be acceptable to Jesus. Because he wasn't "healed" of his attractions, Mark was convinced that God had rejected him. The reality was that Mark truly believed in Jesus and had surrendered his life to him. Because he was still attracted to other males, he believed he was not good enough and fell woefully short in God's eyes.

There is a belief in certain Christian circles that God will heal a person of their homosexuality once they surrender their life to Jesus. Because Mark had been interacting with folks in that circle, he was certain he had done something so awful he could not be forgiven or healed.

Mark was so distraught that he came up with a plan for how he would end his life. The profound sense of rejection he was living with led to an even greater sense of self-hatred and despair. The hopelessness he carried led him to the very brink of suicide.

I told Mark that I was convinced of two things. First, his faith was real--he was most definitely a child of God. He was fully loved and completely forgiven. Second, he would most likely have same-sex attraction his entire life. He would have to surrender his sexual life to God, in the same way those who are "straight," or heterosexual, must surrender their sexual lives to God by honoring his design for their lives. I assured him that this would be both a profound sacrifice and significant struggle. He would need people around him who loved him as God loved him--as he is and not as anyone thinks he should be. He would need a community to support him in every way as he followed Jesus through all that life would bring.

I saw a huge transformation take place in Mark's life in the first few months we connected. There was such relief and freedom in his overall countenance. That transformation came about because he started to believe that Jesus did actually love him and that he was, in fact, forgiven. Mark jumped all-in to the youth group at the church. The other students fully embraced him and provided the community he so desperately needed.

When the time came for Kara and me to leave, Mark hugged me and through tears of joy said, "I think God brought you to Indy to save my life. Thank you!" I lost it in a ball of tears. It was Jesus that rescued Mark, but God may indeed have sent me to Indianapolis to help Mark realize that truth. I'm so thankful he did.

Mark came to me because he heard a message of hope: God loves and pursues broken and brokenhearted people. People just like you and me. I know there are those who feel compelled to announce: "Homosexuality is sin," almost like a disclaimer, when addressing the issue. I'm never sure who they are making that announcement for. Had I done that or said something like, "I love the sinner, but hate the sin," Mark would have run from me and quite possibly taken his life--because, when you are first identified as a "sinner" (as though you may be the only sinner in the conversation) rather than as someone who is made in the image of God who matters deeply to Jesus, you feel judged and defensive--I certainly do.

I'm often asked about my dad's "salvation" by other Christians. My father and I had many, many conversations about life, faith, the damage done to our family, and how to pick up the pieces and move forward. There was a lot of sin in his life to be sure. Yet, I witnessed him acknowledge his sin and seek God's forgiveness. He believed that Jesus was his only hope and he trusted that Jesus' sacrificial death and miraculous resurrection absolved him of his sin so that he too could be a child of God. Though I can't know for sure, I hope to see my dad again in eternity. Our theology never aligned perfectly, but our faith was the same faith. We both believed we were sinful people who had been rescued by Jesus.

SAYING GOODBYE

When Kara and I took our last trip to see my dad in October 2001, we knew that the end was imminent; he could die at any time. Even though I had years to prepare myself for my father's death, it was much more difficult than I had anticipated. It was difficult, in part, because I could not get to my dad quickly from Seattle and I did not want to be three thousand miles away when he needed me by his side. It would take at least ten hours to get to Tallahassee when word came that the end was near. Knowing that I would likely not get there in time to say goodbye caused me to feel both sad and guilty.

As a result, that last trip to Florida to see my dad was brutal for me. My dad's health was declining so rapidly that he was medicated to the point that he could barely acknowledge we were in the room with him. I had rehearsed what I would say to my father on his deathbed dozens of times in my head. As I sat at his bedside for the last time, he looked at me and struggled quite a bit just to say, "Hey, Bud," the words he had greeted me with thousands of times in my life. I replied by speaking some of the hardest words I've ever had to say in my life, "Hey, Dad. I know you know this, but I want to say it again. I love you, I forgive you, and I am so thankful for the years we've had together. Rachel loves you; Hannah loves you and so does Alyssa. I know you are hurting, and I know you want to rest. It's okay to let go. We will make sure Earnest is okay. It's okay for you to go and stop suffering." He smiled and nodded. None of what I said was what I had rehearsed--I chose instead to speak from the heart. My words weren't dripping with eloquence or spiritual insight, especially for a pastor and writer. They didn't need to be; we had already had those conversations. In the end, I wanted to honor him by saying what he needed me to say rather than what I may have needed to say. Watching him suffer and agonize was so difficult that I very much wanted him to be at peace. I confess that part of me hoped that he would die while I was there--for his sake and mine.

Earnest's health was also in a rapid decline, which meant he wasn't able to be at my father's side as much as he wanted and had always been. I hated the idea of my dad dying alone with only his caretakers in the house. He and Earnest had long suspected the two women they hired to take care of my dad may have been stealing from them, which we ultimately discovered was true. Thankfully, the hospice nurse was fantastic, but she had only been around for a few weeks; we never had a chance to get to know her. These were not the people I wanted around my father, nor were they the last people I wanted my dad to see or hear from in this life. Kara and I stayed in Tallahassee as long as we could before we had to return to Seattle. My dad did not give up easily. He would fight off death for another three weeks.

He died the Monday before Thanksgiving; he was fifty-two years old. He died alone in his room, while the two women who had been stealing cash and jewelry from him watched soap operas in his living room. I was three thousand miles away.

Kara and I had family from Wisconsin coming to stay with us for the Thanksgiving weekend. I had to fly to Florida alone, without Kara, to officiate the funeral and bury my father. As prepared as I thought I was to do all of that, I broke down and wept inconsolably as I attempted to eulogize my dad. I was embarrassed for not being able to keep it together, but the weeping had a cleansing effect that was so good for my soul. It was as if I was finally allowing myself to grieve and release all that my father had been and had not been in my life.

The day of my father's funeral was the last time I saw Dr. Earnest Edwards. Something died in Earnest when my dad passed away. Like me, he had many years and many conversations with my dad to prepare for that day--but he was just as unprepared as I was for the finality of it. Earnest seemed to give up on life that day. After shutting down their Tallahassee home, he retreated to their Tifton home where his health steadily declined until his death a few years later.

REFLECTION

While writing this book, I have been confronted with just how painful some of the events of my life really were. I have had to stop at various points because the memories produced unexpected waves of pain and grief that knocked me off my feet. My heart broke for that the five-year-old kid who absolutely loved being with his parents--his heroes in life. The pure joy and safety he felt at Tivoli Gardens in Copenhagen would be betrayed by the pain and heartache lurking just beyond the horizon. I had no way of knowing that it was coming . . . no way of protecting my young heart.

Writing this book has reminded me just how much I have missed my father these last twenty years. I have missed who he was and grieved the presence he could have, and should still be, in my life and in the lives of his granddaughters--all five of them.

The most impressive emotion I have experienced while writing this book has been gratitude. When I look back on the events of my life, there is no logical reason or explanation for why or how I am now sitting in my own home, writing an amazing story about the lengths God goes to rescue broken and brokenhearted people. I am surrounded by my amazing wife of twenty-eight years and three beautiful daughters who love me. I'm blown away that my two teenage daughters choose to go to the grocery store with me--just so we can be together. I am so grateful!

I should be dead, in prison or, at best, a lonely ex-convict. Redemption has made it abundantly clear that God has been looking out for me my entire life. He did not spare me from heartache, from abandonment, or from the full measure of pain brought on by my own choices. I hope it is as clear to you as it is to me that God rescued me time and time again, not because I'm worthy, but because he is love and because he is in the business of redemption.

- It was no accident that I dropped my cocaine paraphernalia just seconds before encountering police officers on the streets of Charleston.

- It was not by chance that I wasn't searched and arrested by the trooper on the Cooper River Bridge, or after our wayward tire hit Big Lar's car on James Island.

- Calling my uncle in Chicago and receiving the news that my grandfather was dying wasn't simple happenstance.

- It was no accident that my grandfather became a living expression of Jesus as he was dying and suffering, by looking past his own pain as his heart broke over the pain in my life. That is redemption.

- The timing of that encounter with my grandfather was perfect. It caused me to leave Charleston just three weeks before I would have been arrested in a sting operation that took down the rest of my crew.

All of these things happened as they did and when they did because Jesus was pursuing me with relentless tenderness. God had purpose for my life--a good purpose, a beautiful family, and powerful story to tell. My story may be unique, but the love God has poured out on my life is not unique to me. Whatever circumstances, fear, failure, or brokenness you are faced with, know this--Jesus is pursuing *you* with a relentlessly tender love. My hope in writing this book is that you would know that God is in the business of redeeming broken and brokenhearted people who find themselves face-down in the despair of their own doing. He is in the business of lifting us up, soothing our wounds, and placing us on a path of great purpose. We need only to surrender to his relentless pursuit.

If you have never been interested in God, or have given up on God for any reason, I hope you see a God you did not know existed in the pages of this book. A God whose first move toward you is love--not anger; mercy--not punishment; compassion--not disappointment. He is a God you can go to, no matter who you are or what you are facing, to receive love, mercy, grace and forgiveness.

Blaise Pascal is credited with saying, "God created man in his own image; then man returned the favor." Sadly, there are times when we view God in human terms and believe he treats us as we treat each other. He is transcendent. His ways are higher than our ways. He created us to be in a loving relationship with himself, which means he longs to give us good things. His forgiveness is absolute--for all sin past, present and future. Psalm 103 says, "He has removed our sins as far from us as the east is from the west." (Psalm 103:12, NLT) When we surrender our lives to Jesus and confess our sin, it is gone, and he thinks on it no more.

What an amazing gift. I hope and pray that you step into that gift, surrender yourself to the God who loves you and to Jesus who died so you can experience his inexhaustible love and grace.

AFTERWORD: Heroes Are Human

As I was writing this, the Capitol Hill neighborhood of Seattle, not far from where I live, was under siege by those protesting the systemic racism that has plagued our country for generations. After the death of George Floyd at the hands of a Minneapolis police officer, the United States erupted in both peaceful and violent protests that represented the nation's deep pain and severe rage over racial inequality and injustice.

These events have me thinking a lot about my grandfather--the hero of my life.

My grandfather arrived in Chicago in the late 1920s, just before The Great Depression, a time when many black families were emigrating from the deep South to large Northern cities like Chicago, New York, and Philadelphia. My grandfather did not see a black person until he was nearly twenty years old.

My experience was profoundly different. I spent the majority of my childhood growing up in the blue-collar suburbs just south of Chicago's city limits. I had Polish, Irish and African American friends. We lived in segregated neighborhoods but went to school together. We were in band together, played sports together, fought with each other, forgave each other, and deeply respected one another.

Yet, as early as I can remember, my grandfather was afraid of Black people. He lived in an all-White neighborhood and went to an all-White church in the suburbs of Chicago. In the late 1950s he moved my young mother and her family from a home in a South side neighborhood near the corner of 55Th and Ashland to the suburb of South Holland, one hundred and two blocks to the South, because Black families were starting to move into what became an all-Black neighborhood.

In the late 1970s, Chicago was plagued by the presence of Nazis who sported traditional World War II Nazi garb and spewed hate speech with the tagline, "White power." I will never forget a march and rally the Nazis had in my grandfather's South Holland neighborhood. Hitler's Nazi Germany had invaded my grandfather's Denmark in World War II with devastating effect. My grandfather had a righteous rage about the Nazis' presence in his neighborhood. He was so appalled that he was moved to tears by their hate speech and racism. I'm sure that my grandfather believed that all men were created equal, and that Jesus died for the sins of people of all tribes, nations and skin pigmentation.

And yet, my grandfather modeled a profound fear and deep mistrust of Black people when I was a child.

The tension I am living with today is what to do with the fact that my grandfather was both viscerally opposed to the racism of Nazis *and* exhibited various racist behaviors until the end of his life. I admit to being briefly tempted to remove the hero status from his legacy in my life. However, my grandfather's inconsistencies don't change the fact that he heroically and selflessly intervened to not only save my life--but to alter my trajectory toward a much-preferred future. If he had not broken down and wept over the pain in my life, I would, no doubt, have landed in prison or died before my twentieth birthday.

I am left to draw this conclusion: we all do terrible things in our lives. We are all in some way the product of our environment. We are very fortunate if our worst moments and the worst things about us are confessed, forgiven, and left in secret. I was not that fortunate. My greatest sins, failings and brokenness have been on display for all to see. Yet, none of that fully defines who I am or what I have done with my life. Even in the depths of my addiction to pain killers, while I was killing myself and wounding those around me, I did some great things. I gave inspiring sermons and wrote articles for *Relevant Magazine* online that went viral. As broken human beings we have the capacity to hold, and to do, great good and great evil--*almost simultaneously.*

"Only fools say in their hearts,
'There is no God.'
They are corrupt, and their actions are evil,
not one of them does good!
God looks down from heaven
on the entire human race;
He looks to see if anyone is truly wise,
if anyone seeks God.
But no, all have turned away;
all have become corrupt.
No one does good,
Not a single one!"
Psalm 53:1-3, NLT

The reality is this, while racism of any kind cannot be tolerated or excused away, none of us are all bad--nor are we all good. We are broken shards of imperfection and inconsistency that sometimes reflect the great evil that human beings are capable of. Sometimes our brokenness reflects a masterpiece mosaic of hope, purpose, love, sacrifice, and goodwill. I would make the argument that the difference, as it was for me, is Jesus--who does for each of us, regardless of the evil that lurks within us, exactly what my grandfather did for me on his deathbed.

Jesus went to his death on a cross--willingly, so he could sacrifice his perfect and sinless life for our broken, sinful, and sometimes evil lives.

It was his love for you and me, specifically, that compelled him to endure his crucifixion. Crucifixion is, in my opinion, the cruelest way any human being has devised to kill another human being. Yet Jesus knowingly and willingly endured that pain with you and me on his mind and in his heart.

On that cross, Jesus looked into time and saw your life and my life and hoped that we would understand that what he did there he did for us . . . so that we might surrender and believe.

Whatever our political, ideological, or religious persuasion, there isn't one of us who doesn't desperately need what only Jesus can offer. I know this to be true. Not because I read it in a book or studied it in seminary, but because it has been the profoundly life-changing experience of my life.

If you have received anything from this book, my hope is that you have discovered that no matter who you are, no matter where you have been, no matter what you have done or neglected to do in this life, whatever pain you've experienced or caused--you are loved more than you can possibly imagine. You matter so much to Jesus. Your pain and brokenness are forgivable, and your life is redeemable. There is great hope and purpose for your life and future.

He pursues you with love, and he rescues you with mercy. Will you surrender to such grace?

ACKNOWLEDGEMENTS

I want to offer a special word of thanks to those who have brought this project to life.

First and foremost, I want to say a huge thank you to the love of my life--Kara Morrison, for your unending patience and support for me and for this project.

To Sophie Morrison for offering the wisdom your name implies; for asking excellent questions and always making me smile!

To Gracie Morrison, the insatiable reader. Thank you for wanting to hang out with me even though you could be too cool to do so. I love your wit, insight and humor--you get me.

To Lizzie Morrison, I can't imagine life or our family without your little self. You bring endless joy and laughter to my life.

Thank you, Lonnie Pacelli for covering this project with your brand of excellence and expertise. I have learned so much at every stage of the process. If you hadn't shared all your experience and thereby revealing the man behind the self-publishing curtain, no one would know about this book. I could never have done this without you. Thank you for your friendship and for being willing to associate your name and company to this work.

A huge thank you to Patty Pacelli for your unending patience in the editing process. At the beginning of this project, Jonathan Catherman, a best-selling author and friend, told me to listen to you and to trust you--"Your editor knows more than you do about writing, trust her." He was so right. You kept me from getting too preachy when that's exactly what I wanted to do–thank you for your persistence. I'm forever grateful.

Thank you to all of you who previewed this book and offered feedback directly to me--even if you hated it! To my colleagues at CBC . . .

- Tom Bell, you may still be reading, but your support, friendship and solidarity only caused me to respect you all the more.
- Jim Wright, we didn't always see eye to eye, but that's why your insight was so important to me--you brought me to tears saying your goodbye, that's how it should be!
- Anne Baldwin, you don't get nearly enough credit for the leadership perspective you bring. You are the truest of friends who asks great questions and offers perfect insight.
- Kelly Curran, if it weren't for you, I'd question whether I had any positive impact at CBC. Thanks for telling it like it is, to me and to the world, and thank you for trusting me and having my back, even when it could have cost you to do so.
- And to Steve Curran, or Mr. Kelly Curran, as you are known by those who care. Thank you for offering your unique insight and for being the one who kept me from referring to myself as "an influencer"! Lifesaver!

Thanks to the CBC security team.

- Ted Robinson, you were prophetic in your initial review of the manuscript. You could see what was coming. Thank you for believing in this work and in me. Thank you for your friendship and for believing in the potential reach this story might have.

To the rest of the guys on that team:

- John Phillips, I never expected a guy, as big and foreboding as your physical presence may be, to have such a tender heart. I love and respect how you see the world, care for the church and speak truth in a way that just about everybody is willing to listen to!
- Chuck Sicotte, thank you for jumping into Rooted and supporting the ministry of a "misfit" like me! I loved hearing your flying stories and look forward to more.
- Robert ter Kuile, I'll never forget our first conversation. Just after preaching you asked if I had called sin "sin." I have so much respect for you and Chris and I'm so thankful that even after that "questionable" introduction, we became friends!
- Derek Bibby, I'll fly with you anytime, man! Not only am I thankful for you and Jennifer, I'm so grateful that my last official act at CBC was to baptize you guys. That was certainly going out on a high note!

Thanks to the CBC Excom for the rights to all the sermons and videos I made during my time at CBC. Your approach to me and to this project made it possible for so many, who may have otherwise not cared, to be curious about this story and supportive of both me and this work.

Thank you to Jim Burns for being a great mentor to a young pastor with sketchy history. I owe nearly every job I've ever been offered to the reference you provided for me!

Dave DeVries . . . thank you, my friend, for being a constant source of encouragement to me--even in the wake of failure. You have the uncommon gift of asking insightful questions that make me think and approach challenges in ways I would never have considered otherwise. It was a conversation with you in July of 2020 that made me believe this book was doable.

To my longtime friend Junior Zapata. What is your job, man? Your schools in Guatemala are life-giving to so many in that country. You travel the world with famous evangelists and to the White House with the President of Guatemala. Yet, you have time to be my friend and to call me, with life-giving insight, when you perceive (correctly) that I'm struggling in the wake of an exit. I love you, man! Kara and I love you and Any--we are so thankful for the invite to Guatemala City you extended all those years ago! (where's my review, man?)

Thank you, Grace Yuen, for offering uncommon insight and support throughout the more challenging days of this project. The world needs more of you!

Thanks to our Rooted group and community group. Bethany and Jason Kennedy, I'm so inspired by the two of you! You know exactly why! Monty and Stacey Chellis, thanks for jumping in, for leading, and for becoming our friends. Sol and Edwin Pabon, you have shown yourselves to be selfless living expressions of Jesus in my life, time and time again. Kevin and Michelle Temp, two of my all-time favorite people at CBC. Kevin, when did you ever not share your convictions? Your love for people and the church is inspiring. Michelle, your heart, willingness to serve and compassion brought our group together. I would break a fast with you people anytime! Amy and Jason Bruce, Dori and Keith Caswell and anyone who jumped in along the way--I love you guys!

Thanks to Markel Croston for throwing the wisdom I offered you, back in my face--repeatedly! Your ceiling is so high! I love you and believe in you, my friend.

Thanks to Matt Conrad for twenty years of friendship through thick and thin . . . addiction and sobriety, "good cancer" and "bad cancer."

There are many others, named and unnamed, in this book who have been a part of the journey. Made For Success Publishing, Ron Rech, Dean Bruns, Ray Lewandowski, Ryan Beck, Danielle Beck, Barb Hung, Deanne Conrad, Tim Clanton, Caedin Pettigrew, Randy and Melody McLaren, Scott Tinman, and so many more . . . .

NOTES

Manning, Brennan. *The Ragamuffin Gospel*: Colorado Springs, CO: Multnomah Books, 2005.

Made in the USA
Columbia, SC
31 March 2024